GuyTypes

DR. ALEXANDER AVILA

Heart and Soul Publishing International

2017

ISBN-13: 978-1544248042

ISBN-10: 1544248040

Acknowledgements

Special thanks and love to:

Antonio, my father, The Great Philosopher: May your spirit rest in loving energy and peaceful joy.

Fern, the muse of inspiration: May your artistic sensibilities expand and create abundantly.

My son, Andy, the Russian Missile: May you be a powerful force for good and light in the world.

My Creative Energizer, Robin Blakely: May the seed of love spread throughout our work together.

TABLE OF CONTENTS

Chapter 1:
Meeting Your GuyType:
The Love of Your Life

ARE <u>ALL</u> THE GOOD ONES TAKEN?

Have you ever asked yourself the question, "Where have all the good guys (potential soul mates) gone?" Maybe they've all disappeared to some remote island. Or, they're all married. Or, maybe, they just don't make good guys anymore.

There's another possibility: Your ideal man—the love of your life—is waiting for you, right there under your nose. He has been nearby all this time. The only thing you need to find him is a psychological map—a love finder that will tell you exactly where he is located and how to win his heart.

This psychological love finder is called *GuyTypes*.

GuyTypes is a simple, yet scientifically proven approach, to finding your ideal man for a long-term relationship or marriage. It is a streamlined, user-friendly adaptation of my classic LoveTypes system (over 40 million followers), based on a unique application of personality type compatibility. I've worked on love compatibility for a long time, and I've come up with a research-tested way for you to find your ideal guy using a method that's practical, powerful, and profoundly simple.

In *GuyTypes*, you will learn which GuyType, or romantic personality type, is most compatible with you in a long-term relationship or marriage. *GuyTypes* is a quick, fun, and effective way to instantly pinpoint the love of your life—it will teach you a new approach to develop a winning relationship that stands the test of time.

Have you ever met a guy you thought was cute and wonderful, only to find out later that he was all wrong for you? It happens all the time, because long-term compatibility is not something that you usually see suddenly and easily, <u>unless</u> you know exactly what to look for.

In my 20 years of research and training with singles looking for love, people always ask me if I believe in soul mates. My answer is "YES." Fundamentally, a soul mate is a guy who is compatible with you in a deep way—who has a personality similar to yours, and who resonates with your style, so there is a maximum of harmony and a minimum of conflict.

No, you don't have to be exactly the same. You can have surface differences; he can like bowling, and you can like opera. But, at the very core of your personalities, you share a like-mindedness in your values, life perspective, goals, and desires in life. That is called being compatible, and is the best research-proven way to build a happy and successful long-term relationship.

THE EVOLUTION OF LOVETYPES COMPATIBILITY

In the 1940's and 1950's, a mother and daughter team created the most popular personality test in the world today—the *Myers-Briggs Type Indicator*®—based on Carl Jung's Psychological Type theory (Thinker versus Feeler; Introvert versus Extravert, etc.).

In the early 1990's, I developed the LoveType system (later published in 1999 as *LoveTypes*), in which singles could find their most compatible mate by classifying them based on the 16 Myers-Briggs/Jungian Types. There are 16 unique LoveTypes, and there is typically one or two LoveTypes who are most compatible with each person (e.g. Idealistic Philosopher with Mystic Writer). Based on years of extensive research with happily married couples and the 16 LoveTypes, *LoveTypes* teaches readers how to identify and develop a relationship with their most compatible soul mate.

The book is recognized as a classic bestseller, and is currently being used by over 40 million singles worldwide to find a compatible partner. Every day, I receive success stories of happily married couples who have used the LoveTypes system to find love and happiness.

Over the last 20 years, I've seen how much the dating world has changed. The internet and mobile technology have revolutionized the way singles meet and interact. Also, singles have become more time-crunched and less patient with the traditional ways of finding a romantic partner. They want to find a compatible long-term partner quickly, smoothly, and effectively.

To help you reach your love-finding goals in today's social networking world, I've written *GuyTypes*. Working hand in hand with my proven LoveType system, *GuyTypes* breaks new ground by combining social networking with psychological (Myers-Briggs) type to help you find your ideal man. In a fun and effective approach to dating, you learn how to quickly GuyType potential dates—classifying guys into one of 4 personality groups—so you can determine love compatibility and begin to develop a long-lasting relationship.

In the GuyTypes approach, these are 4 steps to developing a romantic relationship with your ideal Guy:

1. **Discover and Embrace Your Unique LoveTemperament (Romantic Style)**
2. **Learn Which of the 4 GuyTypes Is Best for You**
3. **Use Personality Networking (GuyTyping) to Meet Your Ideal Guy**
4. **Date and Develop a Winning Relationship with The Love of Your Life**

STEP 1: LOVING THE REAL YOU: DISCOVER AND EMBRACE YOUR UNIQUE LOVETEMPERAMENT

Your first step in finding love is to determine your LoveTemperament—your unique way of interacting with the world of relationships.

There are four unique LoveTemperaments, or romantic personality styles: *Meaning Seeker, Knowledge Seeker, Excitement Seeker, and Security Seeker.* Your LoveTemperament determines which GuyType is most compatible with you—the type of man who has the most natural affinity and compatibility with you. When we refer to your romantic style, we will use the term, "LoveTemperament." When we refer to your ideal man's romantic style, we will use the term "GuyType." For the most part, your best match is someone who shares your same personality type. For example, if you are a Knowledge Seeker LoveTemperament (you value intuition and thinking), then your best match is a Knowledge Seeker GuyType—a brainy, intellectual, kind of guy who wants to make a big contribution to the world.

Here are the 4 LoveTemperaments:

*Meaning Seeker (NF): 19.2% of the female population:** You are strong in Intuition (give yourself an "N" for Intuition) and Feeling (give yourself an "F" for Feeling). You see the world through your Intuition and Imagination; you make decisions based on your feelings and how something will impact a relationship. You enjoy psychology, philosophy, spirituality, the arts, and finding the meaning in life.

*Knowledge Seeker (NT): 5.9% of the female population:** You are strong in Intuition (give yourself an "N" for Intuition) and Thinking (give yourself a "T" for Thinking). You see the world through your Intuition and Imagination; you make decisions based on your logic and analysis. You enjoy seeking information, knowledge, and wisdom—you're attracted to topics related to science, politics, and business.

*Security Seeker (SJ): 49.5% of the female population:** You are strong in Practicality (Give yourself an "S" for Sensory/practical) and Structure (give yourself a J for Judging—or structured like a judge). You see the world in a realistic and concrete way; you prefer an organized, structured, schedule-focused, and time-oriented lifestyle.

*Excitement Seeker (SP): 25.3% of the female population:** You are strong in Practicality (give yourself an "S" for sensory/practical) and

Spontaneity (give yourself a "P" for Perceiver, which means spontaneous). You see the world in a realistic and concrete way; you prefer a free-flowing, spontaneous, and flexible lifestyle (not too structured or time-sensitive).

If you're not entirely sure what your LoveTemperament is (you might see yourself in more than one), you will find out, soon enough. In Chapter 2, you will learn how to identify your LoveTemperament, and understand which GuyType is best for you. By asking yourself a few questions, or making a few observations of your daily habits, attitudes, and perspectives, you can determine your LoveTemperament.

Although it's important to identify your LoveTemperament, you also need to learn how to understand, embrace, and "own" your unique personality—the essence of your nature. Many times, we try to adapt ourselves, and change, for the sake of someone else. This rarely works because we end up feeling resentful, frustrated, and disappointed. If a guy doesn't love you the way you are, he won't love you if you are being less than you are (inauthentic to your true self).

STEP 2: LEARN WHICH GUYTYPE IS BEST FOR YOU

Imagine that you walk into a party with four different rooms. Each room has a certain type of guy—a particular personality style. You have the fun-loving charismatic type in one room. You have the brainy, power-seeking type in another. In still another, you have the family type of guy, and in the last room, you have the artsy, philosophical type. All the men are attractive; all of them have their charm.

Which one do you choose as your lifelong mate?

If you are self-aware and understand your own LoveTemperament, you will likely seek out, and choose, the guy who is most compatible with you—the one who resonates with you at the deepest level of your personality and soul. This is the man who shares the most similarities with you, in the important core values and preferences of life. In Chapters 3 through 6, you will learn intimate details about each of the

4 GuyTypes—what's wonderful about each (and what's not), and how to win his heart, as well as what kind of a lover (including an analysis of his likelihood of cheating), husband, and father he will make.

Here's a sneak peek at the 4 GuyTypes you can choose from (pay special attention to the type who matches your own LoveTemperament style). Also, note that the percentages of the romantic types differ somewhat for females and males in the population.

Meaning Seeker (NF): 13.5% of the male population. He's the kind of sensitive guy you've been looking for, but don't know where to meet him. He will talk to you about feelings (finally, a man who shares his emotions), enjoy that romantic comedy or theatre production with you, and hug and hold you after making love. Yes, he is Intuitive and Sensitive, and often creative.

Knowledge Seeker (NT): 14.8% of the male population. He is the super smart guy who is likely to make millions with his next invention or big idea. He is a Brainiac who is attractive because of his intelligence and problem-solving abilities. He can engage you in theoretical and philosophical discussions, and solve almost any problem you can think of. He is always super-interesting and insightful.

Security Seeker (SJ): 43.1% of the male population. You've found your rock: steady, reliable, security-conscious, traditional, and family-oriented. This is the type of guy who will marry you for life—he is the straightforward, no-nonsense man who means what he says, and says what he means. He is the type of guy who can be your ideal provider, protector, and companion—a loyal husband and loving father for your children.

Excitement Seeker (SP): 28.6% of the male population. Get ready and fasten your seatbelts—the fun is about to begin. This guy was made for your fun, excitement, and adventure. He can take you on a safari to Africa, or dance with you all night at the hottest hip hop club. No matter his age, he has a youthful appearance and demeanor, and his goal is to cram as much fun, laughter, and enjoyment into your life together as humanly possible.

Although all of the GuyTypes have appealing elements (as well as drawbacks), you are more likely to be successful in finding a compatible partner if you date within your own LoveTemperament. As an Excitement Seeker, for example, you are most suited to be with a fellow Excitement Seeker. Of course, you can—and should—have acquaintances and friends from all the GuyTypes (it's good to have friends from different GuyTypes because they can offer you a different point of view).

STEP THREE: FIND THE RIGHT GUYTYPE FOR YOU THROUGH PERSONALITY NETWORKING (OR GUYTYPING)

Now, comes the fun part—step 3: Personality Networking, also known as GuyTyping: Going out in the real world (or using online or mobile technology) and finding the right guy for you based on his GuyType—his unique romantic personality type.

Once you get into it, you will love Personality Networking because it is an organic approach to meeting a soul mate. In Personality Networking, you will discover the GuyType (romantic style) of that cute church guy you always run into, or that sexy Facebook friend you exchange messages with. Using the GuyType mate selection tools, you will determine whether you share the same romantic style (you are more compatible if you do), and you will learn how to win his heart and have a great relationship with him. If, for example, you're a Knowledge Seeker (you prefer Intuition and Thinking), you want to find a guy who is also a Knowledge Seeker (Knowledge Seeker GuyType). When you are both Knowledge Seekers, you will enjoy a more balanced, fun, loving, and smooth-flowing relationship because you're with someone who matches your style.

How do you find the right GuyType through Personality Networking? There are various ways to do it. Here are a few approaches:

Join the Right Personality Network: In this approach, you will join the Personality Network, or community (online or offline) that matches your LoveTemperament. If, for example, you are a Meaning

Seeker, you will join a Meaning Seeker Network of like-minded individuals who share Meaning Seeker values, goals, and deep-seated psychological preferences. In Chapter 3, you will learn about the Meaning Seeker Networks—the places, activities, and groups you can check out to meet your Meaning Seeker (think philosophical, humanitarian, and charitable causes or movements such as The Humane Society and Greenpeace, as well as self-help book signings, art gallery openings, spiritual lectures, etc.). In the Appendix, you will find a comprehensive list of online Meaning Seeker Networks. From within your niche-tailored Meaning Seeker personality network, you will pinpoint and attract the ideal Meaning Seeker guy for you for a long-term relationship or marriage. The same approach applies if you are an Excitement Seeker, Knowledge Seeker, or Security Seeker.

GuyType Profiling: If you are more of an Introvert (like to do things on your own) or independent type, you may not be interested in joining any groups or communities, and you may want to avoid online dating. Instead, you like to meet guys on your own, or in the natural course of your daily life. You will learn special techniques and strategies for instantly identifying your ideal guy. Drawing from years of research and practical application into people-reading skills, Chapter 8 will teach you some of the techniques that law enforcement psychological profilers use to identify their target—except in your case, you will be romantic profiling, and your goal will be to find your loving mate (not to catch the "bad guy").

You will learn how to use "micro-interactions": Asking a few simple questions, or making a few basic observations, to instantly identify your compatible GuyType and initiate a relationship with him. For example, if he uses a lot of emoticons and posts a bunch of his creative ideas on Facebook, he is likely a Meaning Seeker (Feeler and Intuitive). If you are a Meaning Seeker, too, then he is likely compatible with you, and you can start a conversation based on mutual interests and life perspectives.

Affinity Wings: Maybe you don't have the time or energy to find love on your own. If that's the case, Chapter 8 will outline how you can ask friends (or you can hire someone) to act as your "Affinity

Wing." An Affinity Wing is someone who can meet your GuyType candidates for you and introduce you to them.

When you engage in Personality Networking, you will have a much bigger pool of like-minded guys to choose from, and you will find the one who meets your other criteria for a love partner, such as physical attractiveness, education and income level, religious preferences, and so forth. Since you are now in the right pool of candidates based on personality compatibility, your failure and frustration rate will decline significantly, and your likelihood of finding a compatible life partner becomes much greater.

STEP FOUR: DATING AND DEVELOPING A WINNING RELATIONSHIP WITH YOUR GUYTYPE

Once you know your LoveTemperament (and identify which GuyType is compatible with you), and have met your ideal love candidate, your final step is to initiate and create a lasting relationship with him.

In the upcoming chapters, you will learn how to communicate in your ideal Guy's personality language—if he is a Knowledge Seeker (your compatible type if you are a Knowledge Seeker), for example, you will talk about science, technology, history, philosophy, politics, and abstract/esoteric topics that stimulate his intellect and thirst for knowledge. As you gain rapport, trust, and confidence with him by talking about, and doing, the things both of you resonate with, you will gradually draw him closer to you—increasing the interest, attraction, and love both of you share. Eventually, you will win his love (and he will win yours), and you're on your way to a great relationship.

Additionally, you will read about how to maximize your sexual relationship with him, what to expect in a long-term relationship/marriage with him, and what kind of a father he will make based on his GuyType. Knowing what kind of a father he will be is important if you want (or have) children, and even if you don't, his "fatherness" (nurturing and fatherly ability) will tell you a great deal about his character as a potential mate.

As an added bonus, you will learn how to determine a guy's social energy style—is he an Introvert (he gets energy from his own thoughts) or Extravert (he gets energy from other people)? You will learn how to quickly classify him as an Introvert (he may have very few Facebook friends, for example) or Extravert (he likely has a ton of Facebook friends), and you will know how to interact with him, and what to expect from him in a relationship based on his social energy style.

DO OPPOSITES ATTRACT?

Many times, students and readers ask me, "Do opposites attract?" Then, they tell me the story of a friend or relative who married (happily) someone who was totally opposite to them. My response is this: "Actually, research shows that similar personalities tend to attract, and work out better, in the long run. Opposite personalities in relationships usually succeed in one scenario—in the movies (especially romantic comedies). She's a Harvard sociologist, and he's a homie in the hood. They meet in the inner city while she's doing a research project, and they fall in love. They fight (she almost gets killed), they make up, and at the end of the movie, they get married, and live happily ever after. Now, in the real world, what do you think could happen in 5 years when they realize they really have nothing in common? Probably, a split." In truth, romantic movies thrive on personality differences because conflict is what drives a story. However, in the real world, a lot of conflict, and major differences, can tear a couple apart. Typically, it's deep core similarities in vision, perspective, and values that keep a couple together and bring harmony and love into their relationship. So, yes, opposites may seem to attract, but similarities (in core values) usually keep couples together for the long run.

GUYTYPES BRINGS FUN AND SUCCESS TO YOUR DATING LIFE

With GuyTypes as your love finding map, you will enjoy these benefits:

*You will develop Personality Clout: By identifying and embracing your own romantic personality type, you will have instant dating confidence. You will be able to more clearly define and project your special personality traits to attract the right GuyType for you. Instead of falling into the classic trap of changing yourself to try to impress a guy, you will use a different strategy. You will become intentional about being your best self—as a result, the guy who resonates with your style will be naturally drawn to you.

*You will no longer be frustrated with trying to screen out incompatible dating prospects: Instead, you will quickly identify the four GuyType romantic personalities. You will enjoy observing and analyzing cute guys to see which one has soul mate potential based on his unique GuyType. Your love life is a heck of a lot more fun when you can put on your 3-D glasses and instantly see through the facades into the real personality of the attractive guy you're interested in.

*You will enjoy instant bonding and communication; you will eliminate rejection: Because you know you're in the right Personality Network, you will eliminate the awkwardness and rejection of trying to win over guys who are simply not your type. You will know the language of your ideal guy (you speak the same language), and you will become more comfortable talking to him in a fun and intriguing way to gauge compatibility, and to develop his interest and attraction toward you.

*You will stop wasting time and get instant results: You quickly screen out the "Nahs" (incompatible guys) and find the "Yeahs" (the compatible ones). You save your most important commodity—TIME—by efficiently focusing on the guys who are most likely to be compatible with you.

*You will finally enjoy Mistake-Free Dating: You will select the right love partner because you know which type you are, and which GuyType is most compatible with you (and you will know how to find him by being in the right Personality Network and asking the right questions). You will avoid the pain of break-ups and divorce because you will select wisely based on your unique personality compatibility.

*You won't have to look for great dating prospects when you use the GuyTypes approach—they will come to you: When you put your GuyTypes game plan into play, you will <u>naturally attract</u> the right (compatible) guy to you—effortlessly, and in a fun way.

*You will find the love of your life and create the marriage and family life you've dreamed of. In the end, you will embark on your grassroots GuyType Finding Campaign.

The results will be stunning.

You will have all the tools you need to find, win, and keep the love of your life—your ideal GuyType—the man who will be compatible with you in a long-term relationship and marriage—the special man who will bring health, joy, and happiness into your life.

It's your time now: Get ready to meet the GuyType of your dreams.

Chapter 2:
What is Your Love Temperament? To Thine Own Self Be True

In this chapter, you will learn about the 4 unique love personality styles, also known as LoveTemperaments. You will learn which one you are, and which guy is the best match for you—the one who matches your own LoveTemperament.

The LoveTemperaments originate as far back as ancient times, as philosophers and deep thinkers have sought to classify humans into different personality types.

Once you know your LoveTemperament, you will understand yourself better, and you will know exactly the type of man who will fit best for you in a happy, long-term relationship.

Why Are There Only 4 LoveTemperaments?

The 4 LoveTemperaments correspond to four main desires that humans have. The 4 main motivators in life are

*Knowledge (the Knowledge Seekers),

*Fun (Excitement Seekers),

*Security (Security Seekers), and

*Meaning (Meaning Seekers).

Many philosophers, scientists, and thinkers have aimed to classify the temperaments to better understand people and why they do things.

In Greek medicine, they were known as Choleric, Sanguine, Phlegmatic, and Melancholic.

In astrological terms, they are known as Fire, Air, Earth, and Water.

In Native American terms, they are known as Buffalo, Eagle, Bear, and Mouse.

In the Color system, they are known as Red, Yellow, White, and Blue.

In Myers-Briggs type theory, they are known as NT, SP, SJ, and NF.

Regardless of the terms or descriptors used, knowing these 4 personality types can tell you a great deal about the person you are, and the type of life you will lead, including the type of romantic and love relationships that work best for you.

Best of all, by understanding, and embracing, your LoveTemperament, you will become a highly energized, well-functioning, and light of spirit human being. When you are achieving your full potential as a human being, you will naturally attract the right guy for you.

Can I Be More Than One LoveTemperament?

Yes, you may have a secondary LoveTemperament—one that is not as strong as your primary one—but that still has influence over your life. For example, your primary LoveTemperament may be Excitement Seeker (fun is primary in your life), while your secondary may be Security Seeker (safety and security is paramount), perhaps because of the way you were raised.

In the GuyTypes system, we will focus on your main LoveTemperament, the psychological style you use most of the time. At the same time, it is wise for you to be aware of your secondary LoveTemperament (if you have one) because it can also influence your romantic choices.

The truth is that all LoveTemperaments are equally valuable—they're just different from each other.

Can My LoveTemperament Change?

We have a genetic predisposition to a Primary (or main) LoveTemperament (Excitement Seeker, etc.), although we can develop our secondary LoveTemperament as we get older. As we grow, we can also accentuate the strengths (and minimize the weaknesses) of our Primary Love Temperament. Research shows that genetic patterns influence which reinforcers (rewards) we will devote our life to seeking, e.g., fun, meaning, security, or knowledge. We inherit tendencies, or appetites, and the environment we live in shapes their expression.

How Does Knowing My LoveTemperament Give Me Personality Clout?

In everyday parlance, clout is defined as having influence or power. When we talk about Personality Clout, we are talking about inner power, or the self-confidence that you emanate when you are true to your natural personality (your LoveTemperament).

Falsification of Type occurs when you manifest a personality style that is different from your true nature—causing a great deal of frustration and disillusionment—as a result of your upbringing or other people's influences. For example, you may have been Intuitive (imaginative) as a child, but your parents insisted that you become a Sensor (practical) because they worried that you wouldn't be able to make a living if "you lived in your fantasy world." Thus, you became what is known as a "closet Intuitive"—you suppressed your natural imaginative tendencies and settled for a practical career or lifestyle. By doing this, you discounted an important part of the real you, and you suffered from disorientation and pain as a result.

Fortunately, all of that can change as you learn how to recognize, and embrace, your true LoveTemperament. When you accept your true nature, you suddenly feel a surge of self-esteem and confidence that is very attractive to others. You will gain what is called Personality Clout—you have social influence and power, not because of your looks, status, or money, but because you are fully aware of, and manifesting, your personality strengths.

When you communicate and act from your psychological strengths, you are now living from a position of balance, power, and integrity. You will exude a certain aura of quiet confidence that is very appealing to others, and you will attract the type of guy who naturally resonates with your style.

How do I determine my LoveTemperament?

Your first step in finding your ideal Guy is to determine your own personal LoveTemperament, your unique personality style. Your LoveTemperament is made up of 3 major Dimensions of personality, as follows:

The Dimensions of Personality

1. *The Focusing Dimension:* **The way you see the world.**
2. *The Deciding Dimension:* **The way you make decisions.**
3. *The Organizing Dimension:* **How you organize and structure your life.**

For each dimension, there are two options, also known as Preferences. Your psychological Preference is the type, or style, that you are most natural and comfortable with—the one which naturally brings you the most energy and interest. Preferences are usually either/or choices; in other words, you prefer to use one approach, or style, a majority of the time, while using your secondary choice the rest of the time.

The Preferences

For the **Focusing Dimension**, you prefer to see the world by

Sensing: utilizing your five senses in a practical, concrete, and realistic manner

OR,

Intuition: using your imagination, intuition and creativity

For the **Deciding Dimension:** You prefer to make decisions based on your

Thinking: logical analysis and what is just, right, and true

OR,

Feeling: feelings, values, and the impact something will have on a relationship

For the **Organizing Dimension:** You prefer to live your life based on

Judging: structures, schedules, and a time-oriented lifestyle

OR,

Perceiving: being flowing, spontaneous, and not tied down to schedules or structure

You may see yourself in both Preferences in a particular dimension; but, you are likely to use one of the preferences a majority of the time. For example, you may use your Thinking function at certain times, but, overall, you use your Feeling most often to make decisions (you decide by first going with your heart, and then your head. A Thinker, on the other hand, decides first with their head, and then with their heart).

To further clarify what your LoveTemperament is, you can ask yourself the 3 Magic Questions based on the 3 dimensions of personality.

DIMENSION ONE:
ARE YOUR SENSORY OR INTUITIVE?

QUESTION FOR DIMENSION 1:
What would you do if you won $10 million?

You are the Sensory type (Sensor) if you would use the money in a realistic and practical manner (save and invest), and/or if you would use it for sensory pleasure (travel, fine dining, fun activities). Note: The Sensory type is made up of two elements, realism/practicality and a desire for sensual experiences: Enjoying life through the five senses, i.e., sight (colors and textures), taste—delicious and savory meals—and so forth. If you scored in either (or both) of these two realms, give yourself the letter "S" for Sensory.

You are the Intuitive type if you would use the money to invent or create something new (write the Great American novel; start an innovative business to change the world), or to have a spiritual or mystical experience (go to the Himalayas and meditate). Note: The Intuitive category is also made up of two elements, Imagination/Creativity, and a desire to find the meaning in life through psychology, philosophy, spirituality, and the like. If you scored in either (or both) of these realms, give yourself the letter "N" for Intuitive.

Now, circle the letter that applies most to you. You may see yourself in both, but choose the letter that you think is closer to who you are:

S	**N**
(Sensory or Practical)	(Intuitive or Imaginative)

If you are a Sensor (S):

You prefer specific answers to specific questions—you tend to take things literally. When you ask someone the time, you prefer to hear "7:35"; you're likely to get annoyed if your partner responds, "It's almost time to go."

As a Sensor, you like to concentrate on what you are doing at the moment; you don't wander on to what's next. You would rather do something than just think about it. Because you are more attuned to the practicalities of life, you wonder why some people (the Intuitives) spend so much time indulging in their imagination and fantasy. You believe in the phrase, "If I see it, I'll believe it." You don't care about your mate's fancy plans for the future as much as what he can show you, in reality, right now.

In a conversation with your partner, you like to talk about practical, real-world topics, such as saving and investing, entertainment, fashion, politics, making a new purchase, online reviews about the best new movie, or planning the details of a vacation trip.

When it comes to lovemaking, you are turned on by tactile sensations; you are aroused by clean, nice-smelling environments, with pleasing sounds and tastes. At the same time, you can be easily turned off by foul odors, noises, and distractions that keep you from fully enjoying the sensuality of the romantic moment.

If you are an Intuitive (N):

You tend to think about several things at once; your partner may sometimes accuse you of being absent-minded. You are also a dreamer and someone who finds the future and possibilities intriguing and exciting.

As an Intuitive, you like to make connections and seek interrelatedness. You ask, "What does that mean?" You look for meaning and intimacy, and you may also believe in the idea of synchronicity, i.e., meaningful coincidences.

With your inquisitive mind, you like figuring out how things work—just for the pleasure of it. You enjoy talking with your mate about meaning, possibilities, and the esoteric aspects in life—favorite topics include psychology, philosophy, science, and ideas that can shape the world.

When it comes to making love, you are turned on by the unknown, by your ever-active imagination and fantasy life. Sometimes, however, you may be disappointed to find that your romantic fantasy doesn't quite live up to the realities of day-to-day life with your partner.

Here's a table that summarizes the differences between the Sensor and the Intuitive:

SENSOR(S)	INTUITIVE (N)
DIRECT	RANDOM
PRESENT	FUTURE
REALISTIC	CONCEPTUAL
PERSPIRATION	INSPIRATION
ACTUAL	THEORETICAL
DOWN-TO-EARTH	HEAD IN THE CLOUDS
FACT	FANTASY
PRACTICALITY	INGENUITY
SPECIFIC	GENERAL
LIKE NEW IDEAS ONLY IF THEY HAVE PRACTICAL APPLICATION	LIKE NEW IDEAS FOR THEIR OWN SAKE
VALUES COMMON SENSE	VALUES IMAGINATION
ORIENTED TO PRESENT/ FOCUSED ON "WHAT IS"	ORIENTED TO FUTURE/ FOCUSED ON "WHAT COULD BE"

DIMENSION 2:
ARE YOU A THINKER OR A FEELER?

QUESTION FOR DIMENSION 2:
What's your favorite movie and why do you like it?

The key to this question is not the movie, per se, but <u>why</u> you liked it.

For example, you may say your favorite movie is "Titanic."

If you liked it because of the relationships, love story, and the way it made you feel, you are the Feeler (F). You likely make decisions based on your emotions, values, and the impact something said or done will have on your relationships.

If you liked it because of the story, the plot, the special effects, how it was made, and because it made you think, then you are the Thinker (T). You tend to make decisions based on your logic, analysis, and what you believe is just, right, and true.

Although *Titanic* may be initially perceived to be a romantic movie for Feelers, Thinkers may like it for entirely different (logical) reasons. Thus, when analyzing the "movie" question, make sure you look into the precise reasons (logical or emotional) why you liked the move.

Now, circle the letter that applies most to you. You may see yourself in both, but choose the letter that you think is closer to who you are:

T	**F**
Thinker (T)	Feeler (F)

If you are a Thinker (T):

As a Thinker, you communicate to "get things done,"—to improve things. You have a language of actions and results. Your main risk in communication is that you will be wrong, look incompetent, or lose the argument. Consequently, if you feel that your intelligence or competence is being challenged, you will have a tendency to fight back, debate, or argue. And, because you are good at it, you will usually win the argument.

For the most part, you are more transactional than relational. You enter a communication or human interaction with a transactional mindset—having a definite purpose in mind (to exchange value), instead of merely to feel good or build a relationship (relational). You're looking to accomplish something, and you want to interact with people who can help you do that (and you are willing to offer equal value in return).

As a Thinker, you would consider yourself to be more firm-minded than gentle-hearted. You can stay calm, cool, and collected when everyone is upset. Also, you would rather settle a dispute based on what is fair and truthful instead of what makes people happy.

If you're in a relationship with a Feeler, you can get turned off by too much sentimentality and touchy-feely affection from your partner. You also tend to think that Feelers take things too personally and can be weak-minded, as a result. Instead, you prefer to be direct, and sometimes blunt, in what you say. If someone looks bad in an article of clothing, you will tell them—not to hurt their feelings, but to help them look better. You want to cut through the BS, and get to the point; you believe that relationships work better that way.

When it comes to a relationship, and especially lovemaking, you are turned on by intellectual stimulation and compatibility. A smart man turns you on sexually, even though he may not be the typical Adonis. As a prelude to making love, you may start the evening by watching a witty play and engaging in fun verbal sparring (spiced with a tad of sarcasm). Afterwards, you take him back to your place for some wine tasting and an intense political or philosophical discussion—topped off by a jaunt to your bedroom for some heated lovemaking. Let's face it, you know the truth: Brains are sexy.

If you are a Feeler (F):

As a Feeler, you are concerned about people's feelings, and if a statement may hurt someone's feelings, you may not say it. For you, communication is meant to build and maintain relationships—you speak to connect with others, especially your mate.

Because your focus is on being diplomatic, and not hurting people's feelings, Thinkers may sometimes accuse you of not being 100% truthful because you don't always say what's on your mind, or what needs to be said (from the Thinker's point of view). Rather than tell someone they look fat in a shirt (which may be the actual truth), you would rather soften it by saying they "look nice." In your mind, you spoke the "emotional truth," rather than the logical (or literal) truth because you valued the integrity of the relationship, and to you, that is the ultimate truth or reason for communicating in the first place.

At the same time, when others say to you, "You take things too personally," you may disagree because, for you, life and relationships are to be taken personally—that's what makes it all worthwhile in the first place.

In contrast to your Thinking counterpart, you are more relational than transactional—when it comes to interacting with others, you are more interested in the "relationship" you are creating (even if it's only a temporary one with someone you just met) than the transaction with the person (exchanges of value or information). Before you continue an interaction, you want to have a feeling that the other person accepts you as a person.

As a Feeler, you have a great deal of empathy for your mate—you tend to put yourself in his shoes. Because you care so much, you may overextend yourself meeting your partner's needs, even at the expense of your own comfort. When this happens, you may feel resentful because you are not being appreciated for your efforts.

If you're a Feeler, you love romance, verbal and physical affection: kisses, hugs, back rubs, flowers, candy, midnight walks on the beach, and intimate, romantic moments. After making love, your favorite words to hear are "I love you." At the same time, you dislike aggressiveness, insensitivity, and manipulative behavior from your mate.

Here's a table that summarizes the differences between the Thinker and the Feeler:

T (THINKER)	F (FEELER)
OBJECTIVE	SUBJECTIVE
FIRM-MINDED	TENDERHEARTED
LAWS	CIRCUMSTANCES
FIRMNESS	PERSUASION
JUST	HUMANE
CLARITY	HARMONY
ANALYTICAL	APPRECIATIVE
POLICY	SOCIAL VALUES
DETACHED	INVOLVED
STEP BACKWARD: APPLY IMPERSONAL ANALYSIS	STEP FORWARD: CONSIDER EFFECT OF ACTIONS ON OTHERS
NATURALLY SEES FLAWS/TEND TO BE CRITICAL OF OTHERS	NATURALLY LIKE TO PLEASE SHOWS APPRECIATION EASILY
MOTIVATED BY DESIRE FOR ACHIEVEMENT	MOTIVATED BY DESIRE TO BE APPRECIATED

THE GENDER GAP: THINKERS ARE FROM MARS, FEELERS ARE FROM VENUS

Research shows that 56% of men are classified as Thinkers, while 75% of women are classified as Feelers. A lot of it has to do with upbringing and societal expectations: Men are supposed to be strong and logical, while women are supposed to be emotional and nurturing. In reality, this dimension is not just about gender, since approximately 44% of men are Feelers (sensitive) and approximately 25% of females are Thinkers (logical and analytical). Typically, nontraditional types in this dimension have not been looked upon favorably—the Male Feeler has been accused of lacking masculine power (a fallacy, since he can be strong and sensitive), and the Female Thinker has been accused of being too pushy and unfeminine, even though the reality is that she can maintain her logical mindset and feminine style at the same time. The key is to embrace your style—whether Thinker or Feeler—and recognize the strengths that each Preference brings to the table.

DIMENSION 3: ARE YOU STRUCTURED OR SPONTANEOUS?

QUESTION FOR DIMENSION 3: If you're invited to Vegas (or a luxury resort—name one) tomorrow, a work day, would you go?

If you say, "Yes," then you are the Perceiver (P), also known as spontaneous. You like to live in a flexible, spontaneous, and open-ended way that is not limited by time, schedules, or structure.

If you say, "No," or you have to plan it out, you are the Judger (J), also known as structured (think of a courtroom Judge who is precise and definite in her decisions). You like to live in a structured, organized, and time-sensitive manner. You prefer schedules instead of "winging it."

Now, circle the letter that applies most to you. You may see yourself in both, but choose the letter that you think is closer to who you are:

P	J
Perceiver (spontaneous)	Judger (structured)

If you're a Judger (J) (Structured):

As a Judger, you are driven to make decisions—to bring closure to your life (you experience tension until you have closure). You don't like last minute changes, or unexpected circumstances, that affect your social and romantic plans. You think, "If this had been planned better, it wouldn't have happened." The downside to this attitude is that you can prevent yourself from enjoying new adventures that could arise spontaneously.

In addition, as a Judger, you are usually on time, neat (you have a place for everything and everything in its place), organized, and schedule-oriented. When it comes to organization, you like to keep lists—if you do something that's not on the list, you may add it, so you can cross it off. Also, you may love schedules so much that you become unraveled if things don't go as planned. You may even enjoy a schedule (or timeline) for lovemaking because you have the certainty of enjoying quality time with your lover at a specific place and time.

When you're dating someone, you usually don't like surprises (beware of the date who tries to surprise you all of the time). You would rather know what your date is planning beforehand, so you can enjoy thinking about it, and relish the anticipation of actually doing it.

Finally, as a Judger, commitment in relationships is important to you. From the beginning of a relationship, you're already thinking, "Where is this going? Is this just dating, or are we headed for marriage and family?" You want to know as soon as possible where the relationship is headed so you can psychologically know what to expect and have a definite direction in your love life.

If you're a Perceiver (P) (Spontaneous):

You are like a surfer—you make decisions by recognizing the right waves and "going with it." As a flexible person, you may fall into a relationship with someone who happens to be nearby or handy, without giving much thought to how compatible you really are. The good news is that you're often able to extricate yourself from bad relationships because you are flexible and can usually adapt to changes in your relationship status.

On dates, you love to explore the unknown: You like to try a new restaurant, activity, or movie genre. You also like fun, spontaneity, and adventure in your romantic life—you dislike routine, schedules, and time pressures.

When it comes to conversations, you may change the subject frequently—you don't like to be pinned down on things. You like to let the communication flow naturally and easily as you enjoy your partner's company.

In fact, you don't like to be pinned down by relationships either; although you may be as affectionate and loving as anyone, commitment may be something that is difficult for you to do because you always see the possibilities of finding Mr. Right just over the horizon (even though you're presently with a pretty decent guy). You are happiest when your life is flexible. At some point, however, once you've considered all of your options, you will be ready to take the final vow and commit to that wonderful and compatible man.

When it comes to lovemaking, you enjoy sex in unplanned, different, and even risky ways—outdoors, different positions, toys, costumes, and times of the day. You especially dislike the routine lovemaking ("missionary style, every time, for goodness sake"). You like to keep it spicy, fun, and different.

Here's a table that summarizes the differences between the Perceiver (P) (Spontaneous) and the Judger (J) (Structured):

P (PERCEIVER) (SPONTANEOUS)	J (JUDGER) STRUCTURED
PENDING	RESOLVED
WAIT AND SEE	DECIDED
FLEXIBLE	FIXED
ADAPT	CONTROL
OPENNESS	CLOSURE
OPEN-ENDED	PLANNED
FLOW	STRUCTURE

TENTATIVE	DEFINITE
SPONTANEOUS	SCHEDULED
PLAY NOW, WORK LATER	WORK NOW, PLAY LATER
"EAT THE DESSERT FIRST"	"EAT THE SALAD FIRST"
LIKE ADAPTING TO NEW SITUATIONS	PREFER TO KNOW WHAT YOU'RE GETTING INTO
SEE TIME AS RENEWABLE	SEE TIME AS FINITE
"WHAT DEADLINE?"	TAKE DEADLINES SERIOUSLY
RUNNING LATE	ON TIME OR EARLY

Finding Out Who You Really Are: Owning Your Love Temperament

Now that you know what your Preferences (letters) are, it's time to put them together to determine your LoveTemperament.

Write down the 3 letters (dimensions) that you scored from the questions above.

_____ _____ _____

For example, you may have scored something like:

<u>N</u> (Intuition) <u>F</u> (Feeling) <u>P</u> (Perceiving or Spontaneous)

Of the three letters (the three dimensions) that you scored from the questions, you will only use two of them to determine your LoveTemperament.

For example, from the three letters (dimensions) above, you will use "N" and "F." Those are the two letters that fall into one of the four LoveTemperament categories:

<u>N</u> (Intuition) <u>F</u> (Feeling)

The 4 LoveTemperaments, and their two letter combinations, are as follows:

NF: YOU ARE A MEANING SEEKER: If you scored <u>N (Intuitive)</u> and <u>F (Feeler)</u> as your primary preferences.

NT: YOU ARE A KNOWLEDGE SEEKER: If you scored <u>N (Intuitive)</u> and <u>T (Thinker)</u> as your primary preferences.

SJ: YOU ARE A SECURITY SEEKER (SJ): If you scored <u>S (Sensor)</u> and <u>J (Judger</u>, i.e., Structured) as your primary preferences.

SP: YOU ARE AN EXCITEMENT SEEKER (SP): If you scored <u>S (Sensor)</u> and <u>P (Perceiver</u>, i.e., Spontaneous) as your primary preferences.

The power of *GuyTypes* is that, before you look outward to find your ideal guy, you will first look inward to find and embrace your real self.

Maybe, all of your life, the people (and guys) in your life have criticized you for being who you really are.

If you are a Meaning Seeker, they may have said to you: "You're too impractical; you're too much of a dreamer. And, why do you always take everything so personally?"

If you are an Excitement Seeker, they may have said to you: "You're too irresponsible; why can't you be more neat and organized; why can't you plan more?"

If you are a Security Seeker, they may have said to you: "Why are you such a stick-in-the-mud, and boring? Can't you just let go, relax, and live a little? Have fun; life is too short."

If you are a Knowledge Seeker, they may have said to you: "Why are you so stubborn, controlling, and insensitive? You're oblivious to people's feelings, and you always think you're right."

Now, things will be different. Finally, you will accept, and truly love, your unique romantic personality type. Once you do this, you will naturally attract a guy who truly appreciates and respects you the way you are.

As a Meaning Seeker, your mantra or affirmative phrase will be: "I'm a dreamer and proud of it. I create ideas and projects that others can hardly imagine. I bring compassion, love, and empathy to the world. I bring the feeling of the poets, the depth of the holy person, and the inspiration of the great leader."

As an Excitement Seeker, your mantra or affirmative phrase will be: "I'm fun, spontaneous, and exciting, and I'm happy to live that way. I cram more fun into one day than other people experience in a lifetime. I am the joy that shines on all."

As a Security Seeker, your mantra or affirmative phrase will be: "I'm the Rock of Gibraltar; the steady, loyal one who keeps our civilization from crumbling to the ground. Without me, your world would fall apart. I am the glue of the world."

As a Knowledge Seeker, your mantra or affirmative phrase will be: "I am the knowledge and wisdom of the world—the genesis of all the great inventions and creative developments of humanity. I imagine, I create, and I dominate. I am the world's vision and the reason we live in this amazing age of advancing technology."

Wouldn't it be wonderful to finally know, and love, who you are—in terms of your abilities, preferences, and passions in life? Instead of settling for less in relationships, and compromising to be with a man who doesn't truly admire and love your personality type, you will become the most powerful "YOU" you can possibly be. You will develop what is called "Personality Clout"—the self-esteem, confidence, and personal power that comes when you fully embrace your personality strengths and talents. Then, and only then, will you naturally attract the man who matches you—the perfect Guy who is harmoniously compatible with you in every way.

Now, let's take a closer look at each of the 4 LoveTemperaments, and see where you fit in (note: the percentages for females among a particular type are somewhat different from the male percentages in the population for the same type):

The Meaning Seeker (NF): 19.2% of the Female Population

As a Meaning Seeker, your life is a journey of self-discovery—a never-ending search for meaning. Your purpose in life, your mission, is to understand as much as you can about yourself, and others, so you can achieve your full potential (and help others achieve theirs). You place a high value on feeling connected to others (having harmonious relationships), as well as being unique and original.

In addition, you like to talk about things of great meaning and significance: Love and hate; heaven and hell; tales and legends; as well as beliefs, possibilities, fantasies, symbols, personality, philosophy, and spirituality.

Enthusiasm is one of your natural traits—you can get excited easily and express your joy vociferously—others will catch your contagious enthusiasm and will be inspired and motivated by your words and actions. However, although you can live amidst joy, you can't always shake the intuitive understanding that there is pain underlying joy—it is a bittersweet feeling that tells you that sadness is there, waiting its turn. Fortunately, you don't stay down for long as your hopefulness and optimism kicks in and tells you that, yes, there is hope and the possibility of finding lasting love and happiness.

Because you have a strong yearning for romance and love, you may project your own attitudes onto your romantic partners—believing that they have the same mindset that you do (when they really don't). You may invest them with your idealistic view of life, even though they may be entirely different from what you imagined them to be. The good news is that the more you learn about yourself, the better you will be able to separate fact from fantasy in your relationships.

You're also the type of person who can make amazing leaps of judgement based on your Intuition. You may be able to finish people's sentences even before they finish them, and you can read between the lines: You only have to hear a few words of explanation before you understand the complete picture. Some people may be astonished at what they consider to be your "mind-reading," or ESP ability.

When it comes to relationships, you are quite suspicious of people who are cold or manipulative—those single-minded individuals who go after results in a utilitarian or cutthroat manner that bypasses people's feelings. You dislike people who are only interested in the bottom line—making a profit; getting something out of a relationship; using people—because you are concerned that the human touch will be lost and feelings will be hurt.

You are also sensitive and empathetic to your partner's feelings, and you are an enthusiastic and charismatic communicator when you are acting from a deeply-held belief. Passionate and creative, you tend to possess the soul of an artist. You may also be a nonconformist who is attracted to unique things—the type of unconventional individual who marches to the beat of your own drum.

As a Meaning Seeker, you are likely to have a great curiosity about people, even strangers—you believe that everyone is unique, special, and important. You thrive when you can build intimate attachments and share your life with others. In fact, you may even want to create a sense of temporary intimacy with the clerk at the grocery store, or the barista at the coffee shop, because you have a strong affinity for human connections—it's natural for you.

When it comes to relationships, you seek the perfect partner and love. You refuse to compromise—in fact, some Meaning Seekers would rather live alone for years than be with a person who doesn't resonate with their heart and soul.

You crave intimacy and depth in your relationships—you want to talk to your partner about everything—how you feel, your goals and hopes, disappointments, childhood experiences, the intricacies of life. You can talk endlessly about the important things to you—sharing and connecting with your mate in the deepest way possible.

Overall, you dream of having perfect interpersonal relationships that are high above the ugliness of competition and conflict. Fighting and conflict are painful for you—you will often do what is necessary to avoid it by withdrawing, conceding, or even apologizing to others. Your goal is to bring people together and nurture harmony and good feelings.

If you are a Meaning Seeker, one of your most important values is the desire for authenticity—to be who you really are. The paradox is that by fervently trying to be genuine all of the time, you may actually separate yourself from the authenticity you are craving. As you learn more about your LoveTemperament, and embrace your unique nature, you will become more comfortable in your skin, and ready to be a happy and well-functioning human being who can find true love.

Who is Your Best GuyType For a Long-Term Relationship?

THE MEANING SEEKER (NF) is your best GuyType—someone who is similar to you. Together, you can create meaning and intimacy in the world (See Chapter 3).

If you're curious about Dating Outside of your Type, see Chapter 9.

Here are some dating tips for you:

*Focus on the now in the relationship: Don't spend so much time thinking about future opportunities or problems in the relationship.

*Be more straightforward: Sometimes, you're so diplomatic that your date doesn't know what you want.

*Stick up for yourself: If your date challenges you on your views, challenge back. Don't be so gracious, tactful, and empathetic that you appear spineless. Fight for your point of view.

*Avoid a verbal deluge**: You can overwhelm your date with words. When you talk, try to stick with one point at a time—talk it through thoroughly before you move on to the next idea. Don't try to develop too many sides of the issue at one time.

*Avoid delving into their psychological makeup**: Not everyone likes to analyze their identity and motive.

*Develop a healthy skepticism**: You tend to be too naïve and trusting.

*Don't take your date's behavior (if they seem cold and detached) too personally**—he may be worried or preoccupied about something that has nothing to do with you.

*Don't apologize unless you mean it**. You may tend to use apologies to make others comfortable (this can be seen as a weakness by some).

*Don't settle for anything less than a meaningful, authentic relationship.**

The Knowledge Seeker (NT): 5.9% of the Female Population

As a Knowledge Seeker, you like to gather data, study abstractions, and generate possibilities. You have a never-ending quest for competence, and you are driven to understand the universe by asking the question, "Why?" or "Why not?" You learn by challenging authority—you are always testing the system, and you are critical and impatient of others' shortcoming.

You have what is known as a "Complex Personality"—you can be serious and cerebral, but also quite witty and humorous. When you were younger, you may have been stiff or awkward when it came to dating (perhaps even what some would call "shy")—you may not have shown much interest in developing social graces or being popular. As you grew older, you may have become more social and outgoing, or you may have retained your more reclusive or solitary nature.

You're typically not sexually promiscuous; in fact, it takes quite a lot for you to allow yourself to be sexually vulnerable. You like to be in control and you are also a private person—your relationships tend to develop slowly and, only when you find a mate who is worthy of your personal investment, do you allow yourself to become sexual with them. You think through your relationships carefully; you want to map out the relationship and determine its long-term potential.

For you, compatibility of mind is an important consideration in choosing a mate—you want someone who is competent and who can stimulate your mind.

If you are a Knowledge Seeker, you have these qualities:

You are a visionary: You're always looking ahead, putting the puzzle pieces together, even before other people realize there is a puzzle.

You are the Queen of the Jungle: When people need advice and direction, they come to you—you have answers and solutions.

You May Be Perceived as Demanding and Critical: Because you're impatient with human inadequacy (you don't accept it in yourself or others), nothing short of efficiency is tolerated. You have little patience for mental dullness, lack of common sense, and unpreparedness. You expect results and competence—you like people who know what they're doing.

You are Assertive and Determined: You know where you stand, and you have the innate knowledge that you are right. Consequently, you speak your mind directly and honestly—not worrying too much about the effect of your words on your popularity.

You are Calculating Like a Chess Player: You use your logic to create systems for things, and you like to plan out your moves in love and life far in advance.

You are the type of person who tends to inspire trust and admiration in others because you exude such self-confidence.

As a Knowledge Seeker, you can be argumentative, especially when you think that your competence or knowledge is being challenged. Even when others aren't directly challenging your abilities or wisdom, you still enjoy a vigorous debate and logical argument on a myriad of topics, as long as your partner doesn't take it too seriously or personally.

Eliminating error is one of your biggest life projects. You recognize that error is to be expected, especially in relationships. In fact, you fully expect that nothing can be assumed to be 100% correct. At the same time, you're not happy with yourself until you eliminate error. When you play sports, cards, or board games, you must have continuous improvement. When it comes to relationships, you apply the same high standards, and you want to help you partner grow and become better.

You have a lot of ingenuity—you're able to design a machine or experiment; develop a theory or long-range plan.

One thing about you is true: You value your independence and freedom to live according to your own schema of life. You are a pure individualist, and this sense of personal integrity gives you an absolute sense of self-confidence and strength of will. You believe you can overcome any obstacle, dominate any field, conquer any enemy (even your own thoughts) with your persistence and willpower. Your worst fear is that your willpower will fail you.

As a Knowledge Seeker, you have a strong yearning for achievement—you must achieve. As a result of your perfectionistic mindset, you are never fully satisfied—you have a gnawing hunger to achieve whatever goals you have set for yourself (such as acquiring knowledge or wisdom).

Finally, you may see dating as a necessary nuisance: You are not enamored with dating for dating's sake. You view dating as a system for determining compatibility and ultimately finding your mind ma-te (someone who is compatible with you intellectually and sexual-ly)—until then, you will tolerate the convoluted, and often frustrat-ing, dating process so you can reach your goal of developing a mutu-ally satisfying relationship.

Who is Your Best GuyType For a Long-Term Relationship?

THE KNOWLEDGE SEEKER (NT) is your best GuyType for a ro-mantic relationship—someone similar to you. Together, you can build success and ingenuity—making a lasting impact on the world (See Chapter 4).

If you're curious about Dating Outside of your Type, see Chapter 9.

Here are some tips to help you to get better dating results:

*Go slow in dating: Think "Patience is Genius."** Because you prob-ably don't enjoy dating much—you want to seal the deal—you may have a tendency to go too fast in a relationship and scare off a poten-tially great guy. Slow down and take your time; you will find that you can attract the right guy much easier.

*Don't be so absorbed in work that you neglect your search for love.**

*Acknowledge your date's emotions.** If your date reveals his feel-ings, acknowledge them—you may not be the overly sensitive type, but you can logically understand what he's feeling and let him know you care.

*Leave your competitive/debating spirit in the office.**

*Try to find something interesting in your date.** Even that guy who appears "boring" at first glance can have something interesting to say.

*Don't be too quick to mistrust what you're told (you might stifle an imaginative conversation).

*Don't take flattery seriously. Some types are natural flirts.

*Don't tease your date until you know them better. If they get annoyed, stop.

The Security Seeker (SJ): 49.5% of the Female Population

As a Security Seeker, you like to schedule your activities (and other people's activities) so everyone's needs are met. Words that describe you include, "stable," "routine," "sensible," "factual," "patient," "dependable," "hard-working," "detailed," "persevering," and "thorough."

You rely on common sense and may hold traditional values such as preserving family, home, and country traditions. You may be a frugal person—one who is cautious, economical, and saving-oriented.

You are probably good at small talk, especially when it comes to discussing concrete and practical topics such as talking about friends and family, current events, entertainment, politics, sports, traveling, investing, and the like.

Since you are the dependable one, you are likely to be the designated driver for your friends. You are also the one who warns of possible danger ("slow down," "look out for dangerous drivers," "don't drink and drive"). You believe in cooperation and being law abiding—following the rules is important to you.

Morality and values are also important to you—you believe that society is crumbling because people are not living according to the right values and beliefs. Everyone wants to take a shortcut, instead of doing the right, disciplined thing. Some people accuse you of being pessimistic, but you simply see yourself as a realist—you see things and people as they really are, not in some "pie in the sky, Pollyanna" type of way.

Your time focus is often on the past—on nostalgia, the "good old days." You are also likely to be a creature of habit—you faithfully follow the same routines: You get up at the same time each day, drive the same route to work, wear similar clothes, go to the same restaurants and shop at the same stores (for the same brands).

Family is very important to you, and you are likely to have plenty of family possessions (heirlooms, photo albums, and mementos of weddings, baptisms, and funerals).

Your self-esteem is based on your dependability, respectability, and humanitarianism.

As a dependable person, you let people know (or show them) that they can count on you. If someone drops their wallet, you will pick it up and safeguard it. You are trustworthy and the type to shoulder responsibilities and make sure others are safe and cared for.

Being respected by others is important to you, as is public recognition. For you, reputation and social approval matter. You like the idea of being respectable, reliable, and charitable—all the while playing an important role in the social hierarchy of your community. You thrive on having plaques, certificates, awards, diplomas, photos of award ceremonies, autographed pictures of leaders, and photos of your family (you may have them conspicuously displayed in your home). Your ultimate aim is to be highly respected in your community. Consequently, you want a mate whom you can present to your family and friends—someone you can be proud to show off as your partner or husband.

You live according to your conscience and moral values—you use words like "should," "ought," "must," "proper," "right," "wrong," "moral," and "values." You believe that people should behave in morally correct ways.

Although you value being respected by others, you are also not the "show off" type. You may be the modest type who enjoys appreciation when you get it, but you are not the type who makes a public spectacle of needing it. You would rather go about your hard work and duty, and wait until others give you recognition.

Your main focus is "being concerned." You are concerned about your home, job, family, neighborhoods, finances, and health. You are concerned about the little things—doing the dishes, gas mileage—and you are also concerned about the big picture in society: crime, schools, morality. You are the epitome of the concerned citizen. At the same time, you often worry too much, especially about your loved ones, and the bad direction that society is going.

Moreover, you feel good about being a Good Samaritan—helping others through community and church volunteer work, volunteering with the scouts and Red Cross; helping the needy by distributing food, blankets, and toys. When it comes to holidays and special family dinners, you work tirelessly to cook and clean up, and you are concerned that everyone is enjoying themselves. You also like to take care of the young and the old (sick). When you do this service, you may not always enjoy it—but you see it as an obligation—if you don't do it, you feel selfish and not contributing.

When it comes to receiving help yourself, you may be embarrassed or uncomfortable to receive it—to be the patient or recipient—because you are so used to helping others. Consequently, you may be susceptible to burn-out because you are so busy caring for others that you neglect yourself.

Who is Your Best GuyType For a Long-Term Relationship?

THE SECURITY SEEKER (SJ) is your best GuyType for a romantic relationship—someone similar to you. Together, you will establish a loving and secure family life that lasts a lifetime. (See Chapter 5).

If you're curious about Dating Outside of your Type, see Chapter 9.

Here are some tips to help you get better dating results:

*Try new things on a date.

*Don't go overboard in helping others.

*Don't get pressured into sex.

*Don't expect the person you just started dating to immediately like your friends and family.

*Don't be too modest. Let the guy know about some of your accomplishments.

*Don't be too judgmental. If the guy is messy (and has other good qualities)—overlook the trait, or think of it as a chance to help.

*Avoid being overly critical, judgmental, protective, or controlling.

*Develop your spontaneous, romantic side.

The Excitement Seeker (SP): 25.3% of the Female Population

If you're an Excitement Seeker, you love fun, spontaneity, and adventure. Your motto is "Try everything once and the good things twice." Although most people may have a desire for excitement at times, you have a consistent need for a more tangible expression of excitement. To you, freedom means to act on impulse, respond to the needs of the moment, and to have an impact.

You are the type of person who is easy and fun to be around—quick with a joke, laugh, or smile—you don't take things seriously for too long. You are also eager to try out the next fun experience.

Because you are so open to others, you can be naïve and trusting, and you let people come and go in your life as they wish (you are not overly controlling). As a result, you may be hurt by a partner because they try to take advantage of you (they see you as weak). Fortunately, you can move on from bad relationship situations because of your flexibility and charm.

As an Excitement Seeker, you are too busy enjoying the moment to worry about the future. You tend to be pragmatic in solving problems—yet, at the same time, you can be impulsive and spontaneous. You are also very adaptable and flexible.

Because you have a tendency to accept whomever is in front of you at the moment, you may not be good at recognizing true quality and compatibility in a mate. You're optimistic and risk loving; therefore, you may not recognize important character flaws or incompatibility in a potential mate. As a result, you need to remind yourself to look beyond the surface characteristics, and determine what his true personality and nature is really like. In this way, you can make smarter choices in love.

Overall, you are enthusiastic and carefree; playful and exciting. You yearn for freedom and exploring new things.

Here are some other aspects of your personality:

*You are resourceful.

*You hunger for freedom and action.

*You like to deal with realistic problems—you are practical. You ask, "If there's no payoff, why bother?"

*You are optimistic: You like to live in the moment; the past is history (you don't like regrets), and the future is off in the distance, so you don't like to waste time planning for it. You like to be in the middle of the game—now.

*You can be cynical: You can see the hidden motives in other people, and you are skeptical of the "holier-than-thou" type of people—you always think they could be hiding something.

You are flexible and open-minded.

You are willing to take risks.

You may be good at using machines and tools.

You are a tolerant person who accepts people as they are (and you want them to do the same for you).

You love being excited: You have a high threshold for excitement, and enjoy the rush of some new adventure. To you, the action is the prize: You'll climb a mountain just for the fun of it; for the high, the rush. You thrive on stimulation—you live in your five senses. You want the music a little louder, the clothes more colorful; the food and drink stronger and more flavorful. Everywhere you go, you bring a powerful energy; a zest for living, that announces, "I'm here, let's get the party started!"

You yearn for impact: You need to be a potent person who can affect the daily world, whether it be by shocking, mocking, or changing the establishment. You crave to perform impressive actions—making a difference in the world, making your mark.

You believe that variety is the spice of life: You want your life filled with new sensations and experiences. You don't like to visit the same restaurant twice; you want to try a new one—you may change the times you eat based on a whim. Also, you want to meet new people, visit new places and vacation spots; buy new cars, clothes, and houses.

You tend to have a good ear for sounds, and a good eye for colors and textures.

You feel good about yourself when you are artistic, audacious (bold), and take risks. You like to act fearlessly—you may even put yourself in danger, just to prove that you can walk away from trouble, unscathed.

You also pride yourself on being adaptable to changing circumstances; you work well in a crisis. You always seem to land on your feet, no matter what the problem or emergency.

One challenge you have is that you may not always learn from your mistakes since you don't tend to think much about your past—thus, you may repeat mistakes. On the other hand, your ability to "go with the flow" often saves you—your instincts for survival are uncanny.

Who is Your Best GuyType For a Long-Term Relationship?

THE EXCITEMENT SEEKER (SP) is your best GuyType for a romantic relationship—someone who is similar to you. Together, you can enjoy a life of incredible joy, laughter, excitement, adventure, and pleasure. You only live once; both of you will make the most of it (See Chapter 6).

If you're curious about Dating Outside of your Type, see Chapter 9.

Here are some tips to help you to get better dating results:

*Don't be too generous too soon.** You may scare away certain GuyTypes.

*Don't make promises you can't keep.**

*Don't misinterpret a guy's concern for you as being controlling.**

*Don't immediately dismiss a calm and trustworthy guy as "boring."**

*Don't go overboard on pranks and practical jokes (some types may be annoyed by it).**

*Don't assume that someone who doesn't instantly display a sense of humor is not funny.**

*Avoid dating many people and focus on one you like.

*Be patient with questions (especially from the Security Seekers who like to ask a lot of them).

Summary Chart:
How the 4 LoveTemperaments Compare

It used to be called "The Battle of the Sexes," now it's called the "Battle of the Types," although it's not really a battle; it's more like a mutual understanding and appreciation of each other (with a little "battle" or conflict thrown in just to make things a bit more interesting).

Note: We will use the 2 letter combinations for the LoveTemperaments:

NF = Meaning Seeker
NT = Knowledge Seeker
SJ = Security Seeker
SP = Excitement Seeker

How They Deal With Rules

NF: Bends rules, especially to help others.
NT: Questions rules; disregards those that are deemed illogical.
SJ: Follows rules.
SP: Breaks rules. They say, "I'd rather ask for forgiveness than ask for permission."

How They Deal With Money

NF: Uses it to help people—to achieve their mission (they are the most oblivious to money).
NT: Tries to spend it perfectly (competently).
SJ: Spends it carefully; uses money to achieve status/stability.
SP: Spends it to feel free and excited.

How They Behave

NF: Seeks identity/self-actualization. Tends to empathize and seek harmony with other people; wants to be helpful and supportive.

NT: Seeks competence; creates complex models of systems; loves debate for its own sake; focuses on improving/redesigning things.

SJ: Seeks order and closure; tends to be neat, traditional, and responsible. Believes in work before play. Likes rules, clear objectives, plans, and practicalities.

SP: Seeks action, living in the present. Tends to be calm in crisis. Likes taking risks and making and repairing things. Tends to be energetic.

How They Deal With Life

NF: Is trusting, expecting the best of life and people.

NT: Is skeptical; expecting human endeavors (including their own) to be riddled with errors.

SJ: Is pessimistic, expecting pitfalls.

SP: Is optimistic, expecting to get the breaks.

How They Deal With Their Mates

NF: Inspires their mate to be more soulful.

NT: Pressures their mate to be more logical.

SJ: Tells their mate to be responsible.

SP: Encourages their mate to be more fun-loving.

Their General Moods

NF: Enthusiasm
NT: Tranquility
SP: Excitement
SJ: Concern

How They Wish You Well

NF: "Have an inspiring day."

NT: "Have an interesting day."

SP: "Have fun today."

SJ: "Have a productive day."

Now that you know your LoveTemperament, and the best GuyType for you, it's time to delve deeply into the type of man you're looking for. Depending on the GuyType you're looking for (your best match), the next four chapters will give you all the inside information you need on how to meet him, win his heart, and enjoy a long and satisfying love life with him.

Get ready to meet the man of your dreams.

Chapter 3:
The Meaning Seeker (NF): Guys Who Do It with FEELING and INTUITION

If you want a loving, philosophical, and sweet kind of man, then the Meaning Seeker (NF) Guy could be the one for you. If you're a Meaning Seeker, too, then he could be your perfect match.

HOW DO YOU KNOW IF THAT CUTE GUY IS A MEANING SEEKER?

Simple, find out 2 things about him. Ask yourself (or ask him) these questions:

Is he <u>Intuitive</u>? He sees the world through his imagination, creativity, and sense of what is possible. He likes to talk about his dreams for the future and about improving things—he lives for his ideas. He enjoys psychology, philosophy, spirituality, the arts, and things that make a difference in the world.

Is he a <u>Feeler</u>? He makes decisions based on his feelings, values, and how a relationship will be affected. He is cuddly, affectionate, and sensitive. He may even cry at that movie you think is corny, but you'll love him for it (Finally, a sensitive man).

If he is both <u>Intuitive</u> and a <u>Feeler</u>, he is the Meaning Seeker (NF) GuyType.

He is the right one for you (assuming you're a Meaning Seeker too).

WHAT'S WONDERFUL ABOUT A
MEANING SEEKER GUYTYPE?

Meaning Seeker Guys are often deep, philosophical thinkers. They may be psychologists, philosophers, teachers, artists, spiritual leaders, poets, or may be involved (or lead) humanitarian/charitable organizations. They are often romantic, loving, and spiritual. They see you as a complete person—mind, body, and soul. The love you share with them will be deep, and you may even develop the amazing love known as Agape—unconditional love—in which both of you love each other in an absolute, no-holds-barred way, in this lifetime (and even in eternity, if that's your belief system).

As an Intuitive Feeler (NF), the Meaning Seeker guy lives for romance—he is in love with love, and can wax poetic and philosophical if you encourage him in that direction. He dreams of that perfect, ideal love. Although it may sound funny to talk about a guy like this, the truth is that he may be known as an "Incurable Romantic"—he has a restless, abiding, romantic hunger that needs to be satisfied on a daily basis. This notion of idealized love is not something he can take or leave—it is vital to his growth and happiness; a nourishment he can't live without. The worst thing that can happen to him is to have an uninspiring, commonplace relationship—one that is flat, stale, and lifeless.

Here are some other excellent mate qualities he possesses:

He Puts You and the Relationship First: He tends to be selfless, and his first thought is "How will this affect my partner? (He would easily sacrifice his guy's night out to take you to the opera even though that's not his thing).

He Is a True Romantic: He has a flair for creativity and creating ambience on dates with special touches (personalized gifts; notes leading you on a mystery romantic hunt). He is the epitome of a romantic man.

He loves talking about "Big Ideas": A Meaning Seeker guy will engage you in deep conversations about psychology, philosophy, the arts, spirituality, and the meaning of life. He will discuss topics ranging from love and hate; heaven and hell; heart and soul; tales and legends; beliefs, possibilities, fantasies, and symbols/archetypes.

He Exudes Enthusiasm: He has a delightful, contagious enthusiasm about life and the possibilities of your relationship with him. He is motivational, inspirational, and charming all at the same time—able to lift your spirits when you're down, and pull you even higher up when you're already feeling good.

He Gifts You with Empathy and Compassion: Putting himself in the shoes of others comes naturally for this GuyType. He will sense that you've had a hard day at work as soon as you walk in the door, and he will prepare a bath for you (and give you a back rub) without you saying anything.

He Helps You Achieve Your Fullest Potential: This GuyType places a high value on discovering and living his true identity—while helping you do the same. Whether the term used is "self-actualization," "self-realization," or "achieving oneness"—he often dedicates his life to finding and fulfilling his trueness, and making sure that you (as his love partner) also live to your fullest potential.

Generosity is his middle name: He is a giver—he loves to give, even more than receiving. Whether it's specialized gifts, words of affirmation, or emotional support, the Meaning Seeker thrives on giving all he has to his soul mate (that means you).

WHERE DO YOU MEET HIM?

Meaning Seeker GuyTypes enjoy events, groups, and activities revolving around psychology, philosophy, spirituality, the arts, and making a difference in the world. Try online meetup groups (as well as offline organizations) related to political, charitable, human potential, and humanitarian issues. Some good Meaning Seeker GuyType venues include Red Cross, American Cancer Society, American Heart Association, Greenpeace, Save the Whales, the Peace Corps, as well as spiritual/self-help/religious/humanitarian groups and events, retreats, and expos. Other favorites include museums, arts galleries, and the theatre. Also, check out booklover clubs (signings and events), especially those related to religious/spiritual or self-help/human growth topics.

You can also try concerts, lectures, fundraisers, wine tastings, art gallery openings, food connoisseur groups, dance classes, pet shows, human potential groups, and psychology organizations (APA: American Psychological Association). He is also likely to be socially and politically active: Big Brothers, Republican/Democratic/Independent parties, Leukemia society, American Cancer society, and Humane society. If he is more Extraverted (see Chapter 7), you can find him at Toastmasters, National Speakers Associations, speaking clubs, church leadership, political action committees, charity committees, local activist groups, and self-improvement seminars and retreats.

For additional ideas on meeting your Meaning Seeker online, go to the Appendix.

TEXTS, TWEETS, OR MESSAGES THAT WILL ATTRACT HIS INTEREST

When communicating with your Meaning Seeker (via Facebook, Twitter, text, or other social media), make sure you use words that stimulate his imagination and emotions, and that deal with psychology, spirituality, philosophy, the arts, and finding the meaning in life.

Also, make sure you liberally sprinkle some "emojis" in your communication since he is likely a feeling guy, and likes the emotional subtext.

Here are a few sample communications that can attract his interest in you (you can also try your own variations):

"How are you feeling today?" You can also talk about how you feel (sad, happy, etc.), or you can send him an emoji and see how he responds. A Meaning Seeker is usually in touch with his feelings, espe-

cially if he is more mature in his type development. He will respond well to you on a feeling level.

Send him a short inspirational message, like "Every day above ground is a good day." He will likely respond with a comment or share his own inspirational saying or photo with you.

"I love this book" (*or play, movie, concept, book etc.*). He is a man of passion and likes people who feel strong about something. He will likely respond to your message with his own passions.

If you've been dating awhile, and have established an emotional connection, you can message him with things like, "Thinking of you, honey, love (or other endearment)." Unlike other men, who may be turned off by too much "touchy-feely" romantic stuff, he actually wants to feel closer and more loving towards you.

HOW DO YOU WIN HIS HEART?

Stimulate his imagination and sense of meaning by talking about the topics he enjoys: psychology, spirituality, arts, philosophy, and finding the meaning in life. He's the type of guy who loves nonconventional dates: Take him to a "Create Your Sacred Art" class, a fundraiser to help the homeless, or an energy workshop where you work on your auras together. Take a gourmet cooking class together and invite friends over to sample your culinary delights. Also, join him on dates to mentally stimulating environments, such as political debates, human potential talks, or business networking meetings.

For the Meaning Seeker guy, dating is more than just physical fun or a cool social experience. To him, it's an opening of heart and mind to another person—the baring of his soul with a promise of deep regard and mutual understanding. The Meaning Seeker guy offers a lot (heart and soul), and expects a lot in return. Because he is highly sensitive to rejection, and the trauma of being hurt in love is so painful, he may avoid getting involved in the first place; therefore, it's a good idea to go slow if you sense that the Meaning Seeker has been emotionally hurt in the past by a failed or rejected relationship. At the same time, because he fears the loss of another love, he sometimes may stay too long in a relationship that he has no business being in because he wants to avoid the soul-hurting scene of rejection.

If the Meaning Seeker guy meets the right person, he can be carried away by his feelings, giving almost all of his attention to pursuing the relationship—the courtship becomes the center of his world. Many times, the possibilities of the relationship (even more than the actual thing) may inspire him—he sees in each new relationship the potential for finding the perfect love that he has been yearning for, and that will fulfill him completely.

Here are some more tips to win his heart:

Talk About Deep, Meaningful Topics: The Meaning Seeker loves to talk about deep and abstract topics—ideas, insights, personal philosophies, feelings, causes, the search for wholeness, spiritual beliefs, goals, family relationships, and altruistic themes.

Let Him Date Dazzle You: The Meaning Seeker guy has a flair for dramatizing a courtship. If he is a "Date Dazzler" (the kind of guy who puts a lot of imagination and effort into dating you), make sure you receive his ministrations with affection (even if he does go over the top on occasion), and give him props for the effort he is making.

Appreciate His Authentic Self: Appreciation is the life blood of a Meaning Seeker, especially when he is with someone who really "gets him"—who understands his true nature and gives him the rare oxygen of acceptance for who he really is; not what society expects him to be. Also, encourage him to follow his personal/creative pursuits, and to put his passionate work out in the world.

Make Sure You Create a Harmonious Environment: For the Meaning Seeker guy, conflict is painful. Overall, the Meaning Seeker guy will want people in his inner circle to feel good about themselves and get along with each other. He also wants to nurture a positive image of his loved one (you).

Give Plenty of Appreciation: The Meaning Seeker Guy thrives on heart-felt appreciation. The appreciation he desires is not simply based on surface compliments or casual "attaboys," but is a symbol for how much you understand his sensitive and intuitive nature. You can do well by giving him a handwritten note of acknowledgement that shows you really understand his contribution: "Thanks for always being there to listen to me. I love you and appreciate all you do for me."

Be Sensitive to His Feelings: Because he is highly attuned to the emotional reactions of others, and he doesn't want to let you down, he may have a tendency to feel guilty (and worry about hurting your feelings). You can help minimize his guilt by reassuring him that if he says, "No," to one of your requests, you won't reject him or be angry with him.

HOW DO YOU ENJOY HIM IN THE BEDROOM?

To the Meaning Seeker guy, sex should be an expression of "love" rather than just "lust"—even the word "sex" can seem a bit crude; "love" puts the relationship on a higher plane. Although he is highly passionate in the bedroom, he also likes to feel that there is a meaning, and even a spiritual purpose, to lovemaking. He enjoys combining deep affection and caring with sexual expression—which can grow into a lasting, intimate relationship.

To connect on a deep level with the Meaning Seeker, add imagination and feeling to your lovemaking. He's a natural at roleplaying and fantasies. You can be the nurse to his doctor, or the airline pilot to his steward. Together, write or read out loud an erotic love story that you will re-enact in a sexy way—bringing the scenario to life as the sparks fly. Also, he is different from other guys in that he actually revels in cuddling, affection, and words of endearment ("I love you, sugar breath," "My cashmere princess")—foreplay and afterplay will have an entirely different meaning for you when you are with a Meaning Seeker.

Overall, the Meaning Seeker guy prefers a very intimate, passionate lovemaking. With his rich fantasy life, he can idealize a woman's physical beauty (good news, if you're not the ideal body type), and project his own poetic nature onto the object of his sexual attraction. He tends to romanticize sex as "soulful communion."

HOT LOVE-MAKING TIP: ADD SPIRITUALITY TO YOUR INTIMACY. If you can combine a spiritual element to your lovemaking (Tantra, for example), this GuyType will really resonate with you in a true mind-body-soul connection. His ultimate goal is to unite with you in ecstasy—both spiritual and sexual—so make it a deep and meaningful experience both of you can treasure.

WHAT KIND OF A FATHER WILL HE BE?

He is the type of father who will place a high value on stimulating your child's imagination and values. He is an excellent trainer of skills, and is empathetic, sensitive, and self-sacrificing—he sincerely seeks to understand the child's behavior. If you have a son, your son will learn that it's OK to have "feelings," and that "boys can cry" if they need to. If you have a daughter, he will be equally loving and will encourage her to live her dreams (Introducing the next female President). For both sons and daughters, he will encourage them to be empathetic and compassionate toward others, and to do what their hearts tell them. He is a great role model and mentor for teaching your children in the areas of creativity, imagination, and emotional growth.

WHAT KIND OF A HUSBAND
WILL HE MAKE?

As a husband, he will make an excellent companion, lover, and friend who truly wants to create depth and meaning in your marriage. He may have high expectations of how a love relationship should be, yet he is willing and eager to create a soul mate connection that encompasses mind, body, and soul. Deep, sensitive, and compassionate, you will find that the love you share with this guy grows stronger each year. You will also embark on great ventures, projects, and missions together that center around personal growth, human development, and making the world a better place. The Meaning Seeker sees your relationship as an opportunity to create "light in the world"—positive and healing energy—whether by starting (or being involved) in a charity or humanitarian venture, by bringing loving and compassionate children into the world, or by being a bright and smiling presence to the people in your lives. In the long-run, he is likely to be the most inspiring, motivating, and growth-seeking husband you can find—the true definition of "forever soul mate."

If you have a long-term relationship with (or marry) a Meaning Seeker, you will have a source of continuing love, support, and understanding. In the emotional arena, he is without equal. He can bring a special sensitivity and empathy to pick up on your moods (he can tell you're upset after a hard day at work, and he will put on your favorite music to calm you down). He is able to express his feelings to you (At last, a man who can communicate his emotions—Oprah, where are you?).

He is the type of man who will respond to you with kindness, tenderness, and yes, even unconditional love (also known as Agape). He can lend you a sympathetic ear when the outside world turns hostile and everything seems to be against you.

And, yes, he is one of the types most likely to work hard to keep the romance alive. After marriage, he will keep taking you out on "Date nights," romantic weekend getaways, quality restaurants, evenings at the symphony or theatre. He is also thoughtful about remembering important occasions such as birthdays and anniversaries, and he is likely to come up with a special treat or activity for you on those special moments: He will bring your special food, write a song or poem for you, find that perfect gift you've always wanted.

Additionally, he may have a spiritual dimension to him, and you can join him in spiritual worship, transformation, and growth. You can also share his deep concern for the world—spending time with him in charitable/humanitarian causes, such as helping the underprivileged or endangered species, as well as contributing to educational and political institutions.

The Meaning Seeker guy is also an expert in the sometimes-lost art of appreciation—he is generous (another of his strong qualities) in expressing heartful approval of his loved ones (that means you). Since he has a facility with language, he can communicate nuances of emotions that others may not notice. He will bestow conversations upon you sprinkled with terms of endearment, frequent, passionate expressions of love (both verbal and nonverbal), hugs, and his pet phrase, "I love you." Remember, his "Love Language" is Love. To some personality types, his overly affectionate manner may be sappy, dorky, clingy, or just plain annoying; but, if you are his ideal type (also a Meaning Seeker), you are likely to find his expressions lovely and reciprocated.

Together, with your Meaning Seeker, you will create an imaginative and creative home—filled with a great variety of music, art, personal items, family photos, spiritual icons, and books everywhere (philosophy, poetry, religion, mysticism, personal growth, novels, children's books). Both of you may share an interest in interior decorating, gourmet cooking, gardening, playing an instrument (guitar or piano, for example), as well as self-improvement enthusiasms such as yoga, self-hypnosis, and spiritual studies.

On the downside, he may not be the practical sort—so you may need to hire someone for practical tasks (home repair).

Overall, you will find that the Meaning Seeker guy is one of the most loving, dedicated, affectionate, and appreciative mates you will ever find. He is a true master in the art of intimacy—able to see the world through your eyes and take himself into your mental state so completely that you feel totally understood and accepted. For the Meaning Seeker, building close and loving relationships is the most natural thing for him to do.

CHEATER'S ALERT

While cheaters (infidelity) can be found in any of the four GuyTypes, a Meaning Seeker is not one who takes cheating lightly. Because he often brings a strong psychological and spiritual component to sexual intimacy, he is usually not one to divert his emotional energy from his beloved, his soul mate. However, if he feels that he is lacking the emotional and spiritual deep connection that he wants with you, he may "emotionally cheat" on you by befriending someone who does cultivate his deeper, more sensitive side. He may not physically cheat on you (sexually), but he may spend more time and attention on the other person than is warranted. The good news is that it is easy to tell if the Meaning Seeker is emotionally straying from the relationship because his moods are fairly easy to read, and you can take the appropriate steps to open an honest dialogue.

WHAT ARE THE PROS AND CONS OF MARRYING THE MEANING SEEKER GUYTYPE?

PROS: He is sensitive, imaginative, loving, and deep. He enjoys exploring the philosophical, psychological, and spiritual sides of life and love. He will stimulate your imagination, encourage your vision, and help you achieve that ideal love called Agape: Unconditional love.

CONS: He can sometimes seem like he's "Pie in the Sky" or unrealistic—occasionally indifferent to the practical aspects of life. At times, he can be so caught up in his grand dreams that you may need to haul him back down to earth once in a while ("It's time to take out the garbage, Don Quixote").

OVERALL: He can inspire you to achieve your own greatness, while providing you with a unique outlook on life that never fails to inspire—he can be your personal guru, teacher, or guide—your "Dreamcatcher." At the same time, his romantic, loving, and meaning-seeking nature will ensure that you will feel loved like you have never been loved before. It boils down to this: If you want a deep, loving, spiritual, and romantic love relationship with no limits, then the Meaning Seeker is the guy for you.

Chapter 4:
The Knowledge Seeker (NT): Guys Who Do It with INTUITION and THINKING

If you want a brainy, successful, and powerful kind of man, then the Knowledge Seeker Guy could be the one for you. If you're a Knowledge Seeker too, then he could be your perfect match.

HOW DO YOU KNOW IF THAT CUTE GUY IS A KNOWLEDGE SEEKER?

Simple, find out 2 things about him. Ask yourself (or ask him) these questions:

Is he Intuitive? He sees the world through his imagination, creativity, and sense of what is possible. He likes to talk about his dreams for the future and about improving things—he lives for his ideas. He enjoys science, philosophy, politics, and anything else that stimulates his imagination and desire to impact the world.

Is he a Thinker? He makes decisions based on his logic—on what he thinks is rational, logical, and true. If he needs to say something that may hurt someone's feelings, he will probably say it (hopefully, while still being tactful) because it's the right thing to say. His goal is to cut through the BS, and get to the real point.

If he is both Intuitive and a Thinker, he is the Knowledge Seeker (NT) GuyType.

WHAT'S WONDERFUL ABOUT THE KNOWLEDGE SEEKER GUYTYPE?

A Knowledge Seeker Guy is a brainy, thought-provoking, and fascinating individual (with emphasis on the word, individual) who marches to the beat of his own dream. A creative, independent, and out-of-the-box thinker, his personal style can be very unique and intriguing—far different from anything you've ever seen before. This is a powerful man—in his intellect and ability to come up with unique and world-shaking ideas. He may be a scientist, lawyer, professor, inventor, engineer, entrepreneur, or a leader in business and government. As your partner, he will get you to think, stimulate your imagination, and help you solve problems you didn't even know you had. As a lifemate, he is always engaging and interesting to be with, and you can enjoy his deliciously sarcastic sense of humor and ability to see the world from a surprisingly whimsical point of view. Also, he is a great strategic thinker, and he can help create a brilliant blueprint for your life together—mixing in the right amount of fun, growth, and accomplishment.

Here are some more excellent mate qualities he possesses:

He Makes Things Happen: He is competitive and likes to be successful in everything he does. He will go to great lengths to woo your love interest, and you will have a great time in the process.

He promotes interesting experiences: He knows a little about everything and enjoys expanding your intellectual horizons. He may treat you to an afternoon at an art museum where he takes you on a personal tour and explains things to you—capped off by dinner at a trendy fusion restaurant that mirrors the art you just experienced.

He is an excellent provider: He loves to win and chooses occupations where he can excel and be rewarded financially. He is determined to succeed and make enough money for both of you to enjoy life. With him, you can feel secure in your financial future together.

He lets you know where you stand in the relationship: He is direct and straightforward. If something is not working out in the relationship, he will tell you what is wrong so it can be fixed.

He provides natural leadership in your relationship: He has a very strong presence and is very decisive/action-oriented by nature. He is already thinking five years down the line and has Plan B (C, D, and E) ready, in case Plan A doesn't work. He meets obstacles head-on to fix them, and you can rest assured knowing that you're in capable hands.

His intellectual confidence is sexy: This Brainiac will stimulate your mind and inspire you with his intellect—reminding you that the brain is the sexiest organ alive.

His sarcastic wit is brilliantly funny: You will laugh your head off as he verbally punctures the self-righteous, pompous, and weak-minded of the world. His sarcastic comedic timing is impeccable. He can provide a "darkly funny" view of the world that you can thoroughly enjoy.

ARE YOU A SAPIOPHILE: BRAINS OVER BEAUTY?

If you are a Sapiophile, then the Knowledge Seeker Guy can be perfect for you. A Sapiophile is someone who is sexually attracted to intelligent, brilliant, and even nerdy men. For a sapiophile, a man's physical appearance may be not as important as his "intellectual appearance," —his intellect, creativity, and "just plain smarts" (think a Quentin Tarantino or Steve Jobs type) turn you on, and make you want to get intimate with him. On the other hand, a man could be a hunky male model, but if the first words out of his mouth are, "Yeah, dude," you are turned off real quick. If you're a "brain first" person, a guy with less than perfect physical features could drive you crazy for him if he speaks eloquently and has deep intelligence and wit. His raw intelligence is transmuted into sexual attraction in your mind, and you want to love his mind and his body. If you resonate with the term, "Sapiophile," you may just be the type who will truly enjoy the Knowledge Seeker guy.

WHERE DO YOU MEET HIM?

Knowledge Seeker GuyTypes enjoy events, groups, and activities that stimulate their logical and imaginative minds—where intellectual, educated, and cultured people are found. You can find them (online and offline) at wine tastings, chess clubs, music societies and clubs, science and science fiction clubs (and activities), such as Star Trek and Star Wars (conventions are a favorite, especially for the more Introverted types—see Chapter 7), computer clubs and fairs, advanced degree singles clubs, museum exhibitions, jazz and classical music concerts, exotic or antique car shows, used book stores, history clubs, literature appreciation clubs, trade shows, linguistic societies, inventor clubs, entrepreneur groups, speaking organizations (especially if they are more Extraverted, see Chapter 7), such as Toastmasters and the National Speakers Association, lawyer's associations (they are often attorneys; you might even try the law library to meet some budding lawyers), sailing, polo, golf, and tennis clubs, fine import shops, and exotic car dealers. For the high-powered Knowledge Seekers, you can find them as leaders of political, charitable, and religious organizations.

For additional ideas on meeting your Knowledge Seeker online, check out the Appendix.

TEXTS, TWEETS, OR MESSAGES THAT WILL ATTRACT HIS INTEREST

When communicating with your Knowledge Seeker (via Facebook, Twitter, text, or other social media), make sure you use words that stimulate his imagination and logic, and that deal with thought-provoking topics such as science, politics, law, religion, philosophy, esoterica, business, or anything else that fires up his intellect and desire to solve human puzzles and understand how things work.

Here are a few sample communications that can attract his interest in you (you can also try your own variations):

Read any good books lately? A Knowledge Seeker likes to learn, especially the more Introverted ones (See Chapter 7), and he will gladly discuss intellectual ideas with you.

I bet I can beat you in (chess, poker, backgammon, video games, etc.). He loves some teasing (a little cocky challenge). He will be pleasantly surprised when you show your competitive side, and let him know that you're ready to take him on intellectually (and maybe romantically as well).

I believe...... (message him about your viewpoint on a political or social issue, a scientific theory; a critic's view on a book, movie, or play, and let the debate begin). He loves debates, and it excites him to be with a brainy woman who is not afraid to contradict him. You may find him texting or messaging you all night on the fine points of protectionism versus open borders, and so forth. He'll have a great time engaging your intellect.

Use puns and witty word play. You can say something like, "I'm an optimist. A pessimist's blood type is always B-negative." "I don't believe in celibacy for clergy; everyone has a natural biological drive. It's nunsense." Witty and biting makes the day for the Knowledge Seeker.

HOW DO YOU WIN HIS HEART?

The way to his heart is through his head. The Knowledge Seeker guy is attracted to, and falls in love with, a woman who can stimulate his intellect and who shows him that she is competent and knows what she is doing. If you have advanced degrees, specialized knowledge, or life accomplishments, make sure you brag a little bit about your successes—it will turn the Knowledge Seeker guy on. Engage him in deep and theoretical conversations about science, politics, law, religion, philosophy, esoterica, business, or anything else that tickles his fancy. Join him at book signings, seminars, talks, and workshops where he can expand his expertise and gain knowledge. Also, show him that you can compete in arguments and intellectual discussions—while not being too sensitive when he throws in some sarcasm or barbed remarks. Show him that you're not a conversational pushover and joke aggressively with him. Tell him, "Hey hotshot, when they were handing out Phi Beta Kappa's, they spotted you the 'Phi' and the 'Betta'" (Don't worry, he'll love it—he enjoys a good verbal catfight).

Try not to overwhelm him with your feelings; put on your logical hat. Also, engage him in debate (he loves it), but don't take it personally; to him the debate is the fun, and the logic is the game that goes with it.

Here are some important tips for winning his heart by going through his brain first:

Show him that you are knowledgeable; don't hide your intelligence: He is not the kind who suffers fools gladly. If you impress him with your intellect, he will respect you. If he respects you, he will be attracted to you.

Give him approval for his smarts: He wants approval for his intelligence and insight. Remember, he wants to be respected more than he wants to be loved.

Engage him in debate and verbal jousting: He loves debate—don't take it personally if he throws plenty of arguments, debate, and even a little conflict (or a dose of sarcasm) your way—he thrives on verbal sparring and witty wordplay. When you debate or argue with him, make sure you present your issues logically. Be careful, though. He often argues for fun; if you take his words emotionally and personally, he will lose interest and see you as "being too sensitive" (the death knell for Knowledge Seekers).

Avoid small talk; get to the point.

Don't criticize yourself (he will think of you as weak).

Spar back (he loves debate).

Strike up deep, interesting conversations.

Don't take his sarcasm and critiques personally.

Maintain a nonconfrontational body posture: Lean back casually when sitting; focus intently on him, but don't lock eyes (he may see it as a challenge).

HOW DO YOU ENJOY HIM IN THE BEDROOM?

Remember, Knowledge Seekers value competence, intelligence, and logic, even in the bedroom. Study the Kama Sutra and other sex treatises—then display your consummate knowledge in bed (as well as during thought-provoking discussions). Engage in "Intellectual Foreplay": Before you make love, stimulate his intellect—discuss the finer points of Newtonian mechanics, play a competitive game of chess, solve a puzzle together, tease him with a little sarcasm. When he sees that you have a strong intellect and biting wit, he will be more sexually aroused toward you. Also, although some Knowledge Seeker guys are affectionate in bed, others are not. If he's not too cuddly feely after sex, don't take it personally; his overactive mind is already working on his next idea or project—make sure you are a part of his grand plans (and that you value his ideas), and his love (and sexual attraction) toward you will grow exponentially.

HOT LOVE-MAKING TIP: MAKE SEX INTO A FUN AND COMPETITIVE GAME. You can tell your Knowledge Seeker guy that both of you will research some new sexual techniques and activities. Then, you will have a fun contest to see who came up with the best (and most pleasurable) innovation to your sex life. The winner gets the grand prize (whipped cream, anyone?). The more you show you can compete with, and keep up, with your Knowledge Seeker's active mind and intellect, the more sexually attracted he will be to you. Because he finds your mind to be as sexy as your body, make sure you feed his brain desires.

WHAT KIND OF A FATHER WILL HE BE?

He is the kind of father who will encourage your child to excel in learning and school. Chances are, he will be a good math and science tutor for your child (as well as other subjects), and will inspire him or her to explore the natural world. As an Intuitive, he is likely to stimulate your child's imagination with stories and scenarios, and will want to read to him or her (fantasy and science fiction are favorites). As a logical parent, he will teach your child how to think things through carefully and make the right decisions in life (sexual relationships, alcohol and drug use, choice of career, mate, and religious practice). Overall, the Knowledge Seeker father will stimulate your child's desire to read, learn, and explore the world—striving to improve your child's life every day.

WHAT KIND OF A HUSBAND WILL HE MAKE?

A Knowledge Seeker can be an excellent husband and provider for his family. Because he values learning, knowledge, and innovation, he is likely to have an advanced degree or professional occupation such as engineer, lawyer, or doctor. The Extraverted Knowledge Seeker (see Chapter 7) is often a high-flying entrepreneur or successful businessman who can bring your family security by making a fortune with his strategic thinking, leadership skills, and panoramic vision.

As a companion, he is intellectually stimulating and thought-provoking—you will have plenty of deep and interesting conversations with him until the wee hours of the morning. He also has a spicy wit and sarcastic sense of humor that can keep you laughing for hours—as he skewers all of the incongruities and hypocrisies of modern life. His drive for accomplishment and improvement will help ensure that your marriage and children will be an astounding success.

A Knowledge Seeker guy may be hungry for power—he wants to be productive at all times, but can end up being a workaholic. Yes, he likes to be in control, and he often seeks leadership positions (especially if he is more Extraverted). That means he can be a good money-maker since he is always striving to better himself and climb the ladder of success—he is strong-willed, determined, and resourceful when it comes to being at the top of his game.

When your Knowledge Seeker guy is concentrating on a complex problem, leave him alone for a while—he will remain distant until he solves it. When he is immersed in solving that puzzle, equation, or problem, he is in his own world, and is not interested in anything else, including social interaction. Once he figures out a solution, then he will be his usual amiable and engaging self.

He's a great critic, as well. He can find the flaws in anything, including your cooking. Don't take it personally; he is not trying to hurt you—he is simply pointing out what he observes. In discussions, he can quickly pinpoint the logical fallacy of what you're saying. Again, it's nothing personal against you; he just wants to help you correct an error and become better at something.

One important point to keep in mind is that Knowledge Seekers are very independent and like to be in control. They <u>don't</u> like to be told what to do, or be compelled to behave in a certain (socially desirable) way. If he starts thinking that you are trying to pressure and control him, he will resent and resist you.

If he's the more Introverted type (See Chapter 7), he may be oblivious to social rituals as well as absent-minded (wearing two different color socks, or putting on a shirt with the price tag still on it)—so it's good to develop a strong social skin so you're not easily embarrassed by his faux paus.

If you're a Knowledge Seeker, and get together with another Knowledge Seeker, you can be the ultimate power couple—you have a lot in common. Both of you like to theorize and debate. Both of you say what you mean, and you appreciate each other's direct, informed, and exacting approach to people and things. Both of you strive for success, power, and accomplishment.

The challenge is that, since both of you usually want control and power, you may have a tendency to butt heads. Fortunately, you can work things out by taking turns having your say, or you can wield power in your respective domains (one of you is good at paying bills; the other is a whiz at creating systems for paying them). To be successful in marriage, you need to respect each other's power and abilities.

The good news is that a Knowledge Seeker couple doesn't usually require a lot of emotional support systems to perform well. They don't need to acknowledge each other with "warm fuzzies," (repeated statements of appreciation) all of the time—they don't need to spend a lot of time trying to make the other one feel loved (in fact, they can enjoy long periods of time alone). Instead, they are more concerned with productivity and accomplishment. As a power couple, they push each other to be more productive—they enjoy working together and accomplishing a great deal thanks to their strong task orientation. They are more likely to say to each other (and both appreciate the directness), "Just get it done and forget the feeling." As a result, they are not likely to drain each other with "emotional blackmail"—either you do this, or I don't love you. Because they are both independent and self-sufficient, they can almost live parallel lives—pursuing their different interests—then coming together when they want to engage each other, intellectually and sexually.

CHEATER'S ALERT

While cheaters (infidelity) can be found in any of the four GuyTypes, a Knowledge Seeker is less likely to cheat on you impulsively because he thinks things through carefully, and is not likely to let his feelings or spontaneous urges carry him into a sexual or romantic affair. On the other hand, if the Knowledge Seeker loses respect for your competence, intelligence, and capabilities, he may logically decide—after looking at all of the alternatives (and calculating the cost versus benefit)—to either leave you, or have an affair. Most of the time, however, if you are intellectually and sexually compatible, he will lean on the side of fidelity and commitment because it makes sense for him to place his resources in a good investment (you).

WHAT ARE THE PROS AND CONS OF MARRYING THE KNOWLEDGE SEEKER GUYTYPE?

PROS: He is intelligent, creative, witty, deep, and definitely an original. He can help you solve problems in life (he is the ultimate problem-solver), and bring insight and clarity into the things you worry about. You will enjoy fascinating conversations with him about every topic imaginable, and he will have you laughing hysterically at his witty sarcasm and humorous takes on life and people. His ideas can change the world, and bring financial success and happiness to your family—he is the brilliant man that you, and your children, can be proud of.

CONS: He can sometimes be oblivious to the emotional and practical aspects of life (and relationships)—he is likely to forget that anniversary or special occasion because he was caught up mentally in some project or vision. He may seem cold and cutting at times ("That skirt makes you look 20% fatter"), but that's just his way of seeing the world from an analytical and schematic point of view (nothing personal)—he also loves sarcasm and biting wit, so you should develop an appreciation for it (instead of being hurt by it).

OVERALL: He can be a great provider for your family, a fun and stimulating companion, and the "mind" that you go to provide the answers and solutions for life's problems and challenges. His love for you will be analytically based—in that he will calculate your value and make sure that he offers equal value in return—as your mate, lover, and companion. Although he may appear eccentric to some, you will find much to love in this brilliant, thought-provoking man who can solve the puzzles of the universe and motivate you to find your own inner genius.

Chapter 5:
The Security Seeker (SJ): Guys Who Do It with SENSATION and STRUCTURE

If you want a family-oriented, traditional provider and protector, then the Security Seeker Guy could be the one for you. If you're a Security Seeker too, then he could be your perfect match.

HOW DO YOU KNOW IF THAT CUTE GUY IS A SECURITY SEEKER?

Simple, find out 2 things about him. Ask yourself (or ask him) these questions:

Is he Practical (also known as Sensory)? He is the type of person who is realistic, concrete, and practical. He's the one who "Believes it when he sees it," and is likely to say, "Show me the facts, ma'am." He doesn't have a lot of patience for "Pie in the sky" dreams—he is interested in reality and what can be done to fix something in the present moment.

Is he Structured (also known as Judger)? He likes to live in a structured, organized, and time-sensitive way. He is usually on time (or early) while everyone else is always late. He likes to plan things out, and he doesn't like to change his plans much once he has made them. He is reliable, punctual, and responsible.

If he is both Practical and Structured, he is the Security Seeker (SJ) GuyType.

He is the right one for you (assuming you're a Security Seeker too).

WHAT'S WONDERFUL ABOUT
A SECURITY SEEKER GUYTYPE?

Security seekers often make excellent stable, reliable, and traditional husbands (providers and protectors) and fathers (supportive and dependable). He is not the kind to just play around, or date endlessly. From an earlier age than most men, the Security Seeker guy is already thinking about marriage and family—one of his primary goals in life. Some of them even make excellent house-husbands (especially if they're more Introverted—see Chapter 7) who are perfectly content staying home with the kids while you work and pursue your passions. Others (the more Extraverted type, see Chapter 7) will gladly be the "man of the house" (provider), while you stay home—raising the kids while pursuing your interests, hobbies, and charities. This is a man you can depend on for life—he is stable, loyal, and family-oriented. When you're with this guy, you can finally say goodbye to the "playa" or womanizer (unfaithful man). The Security Seeker is more than ready to settle down with you and build that happy, secure, and loving family life you've always wanted.

Here some other excellent mate qualities that he possesses:

He is traditional, family-oriented, loyal, hardworking, and dependable: He can provide a solid foundation for the institution of marriage and family (children).

He is a calming and steady presence in your life: He believes in the motto, "When things get tough, the tough (him) get going."

He is the most marriage-minded of all the GuyTypes: When he says, "I do," he means it.

His steady presence makes you feel safe, secure, and cared for.

His is a great family man: He's wonderful with kids—and is a great stepdad to your kids (if you have any) from a previous relationship.

He is a good planner and saver: He is usually good with money (he knows how to shop for the best bargains and makes sure a dollar goes a long way).

He believes in family traditions and rituals: He enjoys having dinner together as a family and going on family vacations—these rituals can help create a united and loving family environment.

WHERE DO YOU MEET HIM?

You can find Security Seeker GuyTypes at events, groups, and activities (both online and offline) related to family, home, children, pets, and the community. Check out horse shows (and associations), pet clubs, children's stores, activities, and entertainment centers (you can find single parents), PTA meetings, coed softball teams, bowling leagues, county fairs, church picnics and socials, neighborhood watch meetings, condo association meetings, patriotic organizations, health clubs, car shows, chambers of commerce, and military events like shows and parades (military men are often Security Seekers). For the more Extraverted types (see Chapter 7), you can try wine-tasting clubs, beer drinking associations, wedding receptions, sports bars, and business networking organizations such as Rotary Club, Lions Club, and Kiwanis Club. Since Security Seekers are often community-minded, you also meet them by volunteering at places where they are helping others such as hospitals, schools, mental health clinics, and churches.

For additional ideas on meeting your Security Seeker online, check out the Appendix.

TEXTS, TWEETS, OR MESSAGES THAT WILL ATTRACT HIS INTEREST

When communicating with your Security Seeker (via Facebook, Twitter, text, or other social media), make sure you talk about saving and investing, home improvement, sensual experiences (travel, massages, hot tubbing, fine dining and wine tasting), everyday events and news, vacations, material acquisitions (cars, boats, property, latest technological gadgets), and things related to family (children), home, and country.

Here are a few sample communications that can attract his interest in you (you can also try your own variations):

How is your family doing? (or tell him about you family). Since he puts family first, he will get into the topic, and soon you will be swapping family stories (you may even get to meet each other's family members before long).

There's a great sale going on at... He probably likes sales and bargains and may want to join you to do a little shopping.

What do you think about? (Mention a new recipe, video game, vacation resort, gadget, TV show, movie, or news item). Since he likes to be up on current events and everyday matters, he will enjoy giving his opinion on the latest development.

What's the craziest, most fun thing you'd like to try? Chances are, he hasn't done anything too risky or fun (bungee jumping, parachuting, driving to Mexico on a whim), since he is probably more conservative or conventional. This question is an opportunity for him, once he's gotten to know you better and trusts you, to share some of his hidden desires for adventure—things he's always wanted to try, but was afraid to. Maybe, you can bring out his adventurous, risk-taking side a little, and get to know him better in the process.

HOW DO YOU WIN HIS HEART?

To capture the affections of a Security Seeker, focus on tradition, family, and the practical aspects of life. Since he is family-oriented, talk about how much you care about your siblings, nieces and nephew, and dear old mom and dad. Ask him about his family, and listen to the stories he has to tell about them. If marriage and family are important to him (which they usually are), express your desire to have a happy and stable marriage and family life. Don't worry, unlike some other GuyTypes, you won't scare off a Security Seeker by talking about marriage too early (in fact, he is probably already thinking about it when he first starts dating you).

On your dates, try to have everything run smoothly; Security Seekers don't like confusion, delays, or waste. Also, don't immediately try to make him do new things or new activities; find out what he already likes to do, and join him in the activity.

Another important point: Talk about practical and realistic things such as finances, home improvement, vacations, cars, restaurants, and travel—save the "pie in the sky" and "artsy-fartsy" topics for other GuyTypes. The Security Seeker's favorite term is "If I see it, I'll believe it." He wants to enjoy a realistic type of life instead of conjuring up dreams that don't materialize. One final point: Create structure on dates. Be on time—the Security Seeker is time-oriented. Also, if you plan a date, let him know what to expect, since he enjoys knowing what will happen in advance, so he can prepare for it.

Because he values his family and community, you can join him at civic attractions (zoos, gardens, historical monuments) as well as civic events (dinner parties, charity balls, concerts in the park, library events).

He is likely to be the old-fashioned gentlemen type: Let him play the role. He will stand when you enter the room, open doors for you, walk you to the door at the end of the evening. He also likes taking charge of scheduling dates (let him do it): making the dinner reservations, and getting the tickets in advance. He will court you in the traditional way: sharing important family experiences, giving you gifts to show his serious intentions. If you've ever complained about the "lack of true gentlemen" out there, then you can rest assured that you will come face to face with one when you date a Security Seeker.

When it comes to marriage plans, he is all in. He likes the social side of wedding planning: Receiving your family's approval for the marriage, reserving the church, obtaining the license, making all of the wedding plans, inviting the guests, registering for gifts, and shopping for clothes. Unlike some guys, he will enjoy participating fully in making sure your wedding is a resounding family, community, and religious (if you're religious) success.

Here are some more dating tips for winning his heart:

Be concrete in conversation: Talk about projects, events, social engagements, and small talk (he is good at trivia).

Respect his need for schedules and being on time: Be on time for your dates).

Minimize risks when proposing something new: Introduce a new activity, like going salsa dancing together, step by step. First, you watch a YouTube video with him, then you practice together at home, then you take a class, then you go salsa dancing with him.

Appreciate his loyalty and traditional family values: Spend time with his family and yours.

Don't change plans or dates suddenly: Otherwise, he'll see you as a flake and lose interest.

Don't overwhelm him with too many abstractions or ideas: Keep things grounded and down-to earth.

Appreciate his thoroughness, industriousness, loyalty, and willingness to take responsibility and handle practical matters.

Try to have things run smoothly: Security Seekers dislike confusion, delays, and waste.

HOW DO YOU ENJOY HIM IN THE BEDROOM?

A Security Seeker is sensory-oriented, so he will get turned on by delicious food (prepare his favorite dish), refreshing scents, soothing music, and a neat and clean environment for making love. A Security Seeker guy is also among the most "manly" types—he feels sexier when he is able to provide for his family, and when his mate respects and appreciates him for his contributions. Before you make love to your Security Seeker guy, make sure you praise him about his work accomplishments and the things he does for his family—he will think of himself as being more masculine, and he will sexually respond to you in a stronger way. Also, as a Security Seeker, he is likely to be performance-oriented, so he wants to make sure he pleases you, and that you are 100% satisfied (you can also help him relax, and let him know that you will please him too). If you want to introduce new sexual activities or positions, do so slowly—as a structured personality type, he likes to fit things into his established habits. Therefore, you are better off introducing a change in your sex life (position, toy, or activity) step-by-step so he can get used to it and incorporate it into his repertoire. The good news is it that once he gets the hang of it, he will surprise you with his sexual competence; as a hard worker, he believes in the motto, "Practice makes perfect."

HOT LOVE-MAKING TIP: MAKE A SEX SCHEDULE. Some Security Seeker guys actually like the idea of having sex built into their daily routine or schedule—a specific time (say between 8 to 10 pm). Although this may not appeal to some of the more spontaneous GuyTypes, this type of guy may actually enjoy the idea that he has a lovemaking rendezvous with his honey already pre-planned into his day—it's something he can look forward to after the hard demands of his job. When you put a little planning into your sex life, he will be more eager to be with you, and he will be more affectionate and passionate because he has been anticipating your "special love" time all day.

Note: A successful businessman had his attorney draft a premarital agreement in which one of the clauses included sex. It read, "Henceforth, after marriage, we shall have sex three times per week, between 9 to 11pm, Eastern Standard Time." After marriage, both he and his wife loved the arrangement—they knew they always had "their lovemaking time" built into their busy lives. After the chores were done, and the kids were put to sleep, it was time to "get their groove on." Since they were both Security-Seekers, they were very happy with their love schedule.

WHAT KIND OF A FATHER WILL HE BE?

He is the rock-solid dad who will always be there for his kids. To him, his children are his prize and glory in life. He will dote on them, join them in their sporting events and extracurricular activities (he may even be the coach or volunteer), and provide everything they need in the material and financial sense. He will also be there to provide guidance and advice as your children face the challenges of growing up. He can be strict at times, but he will make sure your children learn, from an early age, how to develop good values and habits—with a strong emphasis on organization, cleanliness, hard work, and respect. The Security Seeker will make sure your children grow up to be positive, productive, and useful people who contribute to society.

WHAT KIND OF A HUSBAND WILL HE MAKE?

This is the type of guy you can marry for life. As a Security Seeker, he places a high value on loyalty, responsibility, and commitment. He is a hard worker and good provider—he will sacrifice everything for the family he loves. The Security Seeker is the type of man with whom you can have the proverbial house with the white picket fence, charming and happy children, and a joyful dog (or other four-legged creature). He expresses his love for you by taking care of you, providing for you, and making sure you feel loved, safe, and secure. If he needs to fight a burglar, mano a mano, he will do it to protect you. If you need something fixed, a practical problem to be solved, or an obstacle you can't seem to overcome, he will be there to help guide you through it, step by step. He is your ultimate protector, lover, and provider.

He is a helpmate who is more than ready to roll up his sleeves and work with you—side by side—building a comfortable and stable family life.

He is also a great family person—who worries a lot about the family: He may keep in constant contact with you and the children to make sure you are safe and cared for.

The Security Seeker communicates with both a nurturing and critical attitude—he feels a responsibility for seeing that you and the children are safe and well-provided for, while at the same time wanting to make sure his family "does the right thing," and "doesn't do the wrong thing." In this way, the Security Seeker serves as a moral guide, much like Freud's Super-ego concept.

If it fits the family's needs, he can happily be a stay-at-home dad. He can be perfectly comfortable with doing household chores (cooking, taking care of the kids, taking them to games or recitals). He is the ultimate family man, and he is almost incapable of refusing added responsibility. If there's a job to be done (even if he comes home exhausted from work), he'll do it.

The good news is that he is the most marriage-minded of all the GuyTypes. After all the marriage ceremonies have been observed, he will get down to the serious business of establishing a home and family, cultivating a circle of friends, making social connections, and getting ahead in his career. He actually likes the certainty and predictability of married life more than the constant change of dating.

He is content to live within a routine—he rarely complains of boredom—he may dine with you at the same restaurant every Saturday night, visit the same vacation spot each year, participate in the same bowling league. To him, routine is not boring, but simply serves as a safety net that gives him the freedom to explore what he wants in life while still feeling safe and comfortable.

As a family-oriented guy, he likes to keep up with the family—entertaining relatives in holiday customs (Thanksgiving Turkey), listening to, and recounting, favorite family stories. He also likes to belong to traditional civic groups (Chamber of Commerce, Lions Club), school, community, and church-related activities (PTA fundraisers, father's club pancake breakfast, volunteer for March of Dimes, volunteer at the church).

Another plus: He is usually good with money (great saver with a strict budget; a planner for the future with insurance policies,

401(k)s, savings accounts, and government bonds). He understands safe investments and wants to make sure his family is well-taken care of should something happen to him (he will buy the burial plots early). He is also handy around the house—knowing how to fix and replace things—instead of having to shell out money for a handyman (another waste of money in his eyes).

He enjoys family time—playing games together as a family, eating together at the dinner table, and swapping stories. The mandatory dog (Fido) with the wagging tail will also be at the dinner table, making it a fun adventure for all.

On the downside, his strong focus on the children and family events may take away from his romantic attentions to you, and that side of your relationship may suffer (unless you remind him with a tap on the head: "Hey, when was the last time we went out for a date night?"). He will usually give you the romantic fix you need once you put it in the context of enhancing the marriage he treasures.

CHEATER'S ALERT

While cheaters (infidelity) can be found in any of the four GuyTypes, a Security Seeker is less likely to cheat than other types because doing so would jeopardize the family unit he loves (and separate him from his beloved children). However, things can change if he believes he is in an "empty marriage" (no love or unsatisfying sex)—in that case, he may try to keep the family structure intact, while having a side relationship. In fact, if he does have a cheating tendency, he is more likely than other types to stay married while having a mistress because he will do everything to preserve the appearance of stability and a marriage structure (even if divorce is a better alternative).

WHAT ARE THE PROS AND CONS OF MARRYING THE SECURITY SEEKER GUYTYPE?

PROS: He is manly, protective, practical, organized, gentlemanly, and family-oriented—he is able to get things done. Also, he enjoys the sensory aspects of life—fine wine, dining, travel, sensual experiences—as long as they are reasonable in time, energy, and money. You will feel safe and comfortable with him as you build a family together.

CONS: Some Security Seekers may not be as affectionate as you may like—they may even appear dry and cold at times—more focused on practical matters such as paying the bills instead of giving you a hug. Also, their emphasis on organization and structure may seem burdensome at times—they can also be tight with money due to their practical nature. You may be tempted to say to him, "Come, on, let loose and have a little fun; you've already calculated the cost of the vacation to the last penny. Let's splurge a little—you only live once."

OVERALL: He can be the ultimate life mate and family man you've always dreamed of. Instead of having to convince a man to commit to you, he is already halfway there as soon as he starts dating you. He wants to build a successful marriage and family life with you—including children—either your own, adopted ones, or even grandchildren (depending on your age). More good news: As a hard-working provider, he will make sure your family has financial stability, and he will offer you a sense of protection, security, and comfort. You know he will always be there for you—he will always have your back. The right Security Seeker can be your knight in shining armor who fights battles for you, brings home the bacon, and loves you and your family for a lifetime.

Chapter 6:
The Excitement Seeker (SP): Guys Who Do It with SENSATION and SPONTANEITY

If you want an exciting, spontaneous, fun-loving, "go for the gusto" kind of man, then the Excitement Seeker Guy could be the one for you. If you're an Excitement Seeker too, then he could be your perfect match.

HOW DO YOU KNOW IF THAT CUTE GUY IS AN EXCITEMENT SEEKER?

Simple, find out 2 things about him. Ask yourself (or ask him) these questions:

Is he <u>Practical (also known as Sensory)</u>? He is the type of person who sees the world in a realistic and concrete way. He is also a sensualist; he is attracted to the sensory pleasures of life—fine food, drink, travel, lovemaking, music, friendship, nature, and laughter.

Is he <u>Spontaneous (also known as Perceiver)</u>? He organizes his life in a free-flowing spontaneous way that is not tied to time-rigid schedules and repetitive structure. He is fun-loving, easy-going, and playful—he is always ready for any adventure you may suggest.

If he is both <u>Practical</u> and <u>Spontaneous</u>, he is the Excitement Seeker (SP) GuyType.

He is the right one for you (assuming you're an Excitement Seeker, too).

WHAT'S WONDERFUL ABOUT AN EXCITEMENT SEEKER GUYTYPE?

His middle name is excitement. He was created to bring fun, spontaneity, excitement, and adventure into your life. The Excitement Seeker is the definition of the fun companion who will always keep you laughing, excited, thrilled, stimulated, and "hot" for him and whatever adventure or activity he has planned for you next. Yes, he is also exciting in bed—ready to try new positions, places, or scenarios in lovemaking. And the more Extraverted he is (See Chapter 7), the more likely he is to bring you a ready-made social life—chock-full of friends and social networking and party (fun) opportunities.

When you're with the Excitement Seeker, you will decide that life is, indeed, an amazing party. He represents the spirit of the wind—spirited, exciting, and with an innate ability to be happy.

Here are some excellent benefits that he brings to the table:

He is great fun to be around, and you will make friends just by being around him: His charismatic nature makes him popular, and he is able to charm elderly people in stores as well as babies in strollers.

He can be an amazing marketer, salesperson, and promoter (especially the more Extraverted type—see Chapter 7): He can sell sand to desert dwellers. As a result, he can be very productive and financially successful (you will enjoy an extravagant lifestyle) if he chooses a career in persuasion or business.

He doesn't seek to control others (and doesn't want to be controlled): He likes to relate to others in an open, spontaneous, and carefree manner.

He loves surprises (and he loves to give them): He loves to celebrate everything imaginable—holidays and special moments. If there's not a special occasion handy, he'll create one, such as "I'm alive day." He's likely to say, "As long as I'm still breathing, then it's time to celebrate."

He is one of the most generous of the GuyTypes: He loves to bring you flowers, candy, special gifts—whisking you off to exotic locations and fun events; he may even throw you a party, just for the heck of it. He loves to surprise you with his gifts.

He is the ultimate playmate: He will lighten your mood when you're sad or grumpy, and devote himself to your pleasure and excitement, in the bedroom, and outside. He is a pleasure seeker and a pleasure giver.

He is a die-hard optimist: He would rather appreciate what he has than be miserable about what he lacks—he is filled with confidence that the best is yet to come. Because he is often optimistic, he is usually the recipient of good luck. In fact, research has found that optimists tend to have better luck—they get involved in better relationships, have better jobs, make more money, and do better with their choices in life.

With him leading the way, the two of you can enjoy dancing, nightclubs, parties, casinos, comedy clubs, grand openings, nature adventures (white river rafting), thrill-seeking activities (parachuting, bungie jumping, paintballing, shooting guns at the range), and the like. He is also likely to be a great salesmen or marketer (especially if he is more Extraverted) who can bring plenty of money to the table through his work activities. Remember this about the Excitement Seeker GuyType: Excitement is his middle name, and fun and adventure are his games—get ready to join the fun!

WHERE DO YOU MEET HIM?

You can meet the more Introverted (see Chapter 7) Excitement Seeker GuyType at events, groups, and activities (online and offline) that revolve around his interests and hobbies related to art, nature, crafts, and outdoor adventures. You can look into gardening clubs, animal rights organizations (such as PETA), craft shops and fairs, environmental protection groups, Nature Singles, Art displays and galleries, car shows, farming-related organizations, automotive repair classes, auto racing, hardware stores, sports, extreme sports, sports bars, skiing, surfing, gun shops and clubs, car clubs, motorcycle clubs, and hiking clubs. For the more Extraverted Excitement Seeker, you can find him at bars, swing dance clubs, comedy clubs, night-clubs, dance classes, parties, gambling resorts, theaters, salsa clubs, hip hop clubs, acting classes, horse races, restaurants, happy hours, athletic events, house parties, and clubs and organizations that deal with entrepreneurship, promotion, marketing, and public relations.

For additional ideas on meeting your Excitement Seeker online, check out the Appendix.

TEXTS, TWEETS, OR MESSAGES THAT WILL ATTRACT HIS INTEREST

When communicating with your Excitement Seeker (via Facebook, Twitter, text, or other social media), make sure you discuss topics related to action-oriented activities (kayaking, boating, surfing, ski-ing, hunting, off-roading), as well as social fun, especially if he is more Extraverted (parties, concerts, comedy clubs, resorts, dance clubs, charity events, live music, theatre).

Here are a few sample communications that can attract his interest in you (you can also try your own variations):

What are you doing for fun this weekend? You can also mention what you like to do for fun on the weekends. He loves fun, and he may just invite you along for the ride (parties or outdoor activities, and so forth).

Ask him for a suggestion on a new activity (restaurant, movie theatre, social activity, or outdoor adventure). Again, he may be excited to tell you, and may want you to join him in the new activity. Or, if you're a little bold, you can ask him to join you.

Have fun with a little stylistic wording, and say something like, "What's crackalackin'?" He is likely to enjoy your hip sense of humor and fire back with some fun banter, "Mr. Roboto, ready for takeoff."

After you've dated for a while, he will love messages from you that intrigue his sensual appetite, like, "I'm wearing a whole bunch of nothing," and "My birthday suit just arrived." He'll love the sensual and sexual tension you create with your words, leading up the moment of romantic ecstasy.

HOW DO YOU WIN HIS HEART?

Dating the Excitement Seeker is like taking a magical vacation to a beautiful island. Get in touch with your fun-loving, spontaneous side—act like a little kid who wants to explore and enjoy life. Take him on dates that revolve around experiencing things—winetasting, boogie boarding, off-roading, hunting, fishing, dancing, kayaking, parachuting, hot air balloon riding, horseback riding. Remember: He is an action guy, and he probably enjoys nature and outdoor activities—show them that you can be a great outdoor adventure buddy, and show interest in his hobbies. If he is more Extraverted, join him on his social outings—concerts, nightclubs, comedy clubs, parties, and networking events—he will grow attached to you if he sees that you're all in for the fun and social enjoyment.

One important tip: Avoid being jealous or possessive. He loves his independence and sometimes can be a natural flirt (especially if he is more Extraverted, see Chapter 7). Let him talk to others without appearing jealous, and you will win Excitement Seeker points—he will respect you as someone who is secure enough to let him be himself. Although some Excitement Seekers may tend toward promiscuity, it's true that he can be faithful and loyal if you allow him the flexibility and freedom to explore his environment without you becoming overly dependent or needy.

Along the same lines, be careful about mentioning the "C" word (commitment) too early in the relationship. As a free spirit, the Excitement Seeker guy doesn't like the notion of being "tied down," or "trapped" into something—he can be resistant to what he views as a forced commitment or relationship. He does, however, love the idea of having an "adventure partner" or "partner in fun" who can join him in life's journey. If you can get him to see you as "an adventure connection" or a "fun partnership," then you can ease his concerns about losing his freedom—he will fall in love with you and will want to spend the rest of his life with you. Think paradoxically: The less you demand commitment from him, the more he will be committed to you—not just by words, but by his actions, behaviors, and love for you.

There is another paradox with the Excitement Seeker: On one hand, you don't want to push too fast for a commitment; on the other hand, you don't want a relationship to drag on too long, so that he gets too comfortable, and even bored with it. Since he is driven by actions and impulses, you might consider eloping to Vegas, or have a quickie wedding if you feel the time is right, and he is ready to settle down. He will love the excitement and spontaneity of your marriage adventure (you can have a more traditional marriage ceremony later once you tie the knot the first time).

When making a request of him, give him some choices or alternatives, then let go of your own expectations. He wants to do things in his own way, in his own time. Also, avoid too much analyzing, processing of feelings, or discussing theories and abstractions. Finally, don't overwhelm him with a lot of issues. Pinpoint one issue to talk about, and then discuss it while you are walking or engaging in some physical activity (golf or tennis)—he thinks better when he's active.

Here are some tips to win the Excitement Seeker's Love:

Try new things and stay flexible: For the Excitement Seeker, "Boring is a misdemeanor."

Be positive and proactive with him.

Accept his playful teasing.

Engage in fun, physical activities with him: Play tennis, fly a kite, go horseback riding.

Enjoy his charismatic innocence.

Don't push him too intensely, and don't pressure him to dwell on problems.

Don't totally control his schedule or consume his time.

HOW DO YOU ENJOY HIM IN THE BEDROOM?

If you crave passion, fun, excitement, and variety in your lovemaking, then you've come to the right place—the Excitement Seeker guy may just be your perfect lover. The first thing to recognize is that he loves spontaneity in his lovemaking—he abhors routine sex (put "missionary style" on vacation for a while). If you've ever wanted to try an outdoor lovemaking adventure (in the mountains or beach; on a tree or swing), then this is the guy for you. He's willing to try almost anything once, and the good things twice (or more), as long as both of you enjoy the experience and have multiple orgasms. He is also a sensualist par excellence—when it comes to sexual fun, he thoroughly enjoys the sights (mirrors, anyone?), sounds (moans and pet names), tastes (flavored lotions), and touches (massages, candle wax), and smells (pleasant aromas, incense, scented candles) of the "sublime act." The good news is that he is likely to have good technique in lovemaking since he probably has plenty of experience under his belt (especially the more Extraverted ones [see Chapter 7], who are well-skilled in the art of seduction). Let him use his expertise and experience to take you to new heights of ecstasy and fulfillment.

This GuyType is one of the most sexualized: He cares about looking sexy, and he will put extra time into developing his body—keeping in shape—and dressing "hot" to exude attractiveness. He is also a natural flirt (especially if he is more Extraverted)—he will flirt with you, and tease you, as a prelude to making love. He is sexually ambitious, and enjoys talking about sex—he is likely to have an extensive repertoire of sexual stories.

HOT LOVE-MAKING TIP: Plan a pre-date to the adult intimacy shop. If you encourage him, the Excitement Seeker guy will love to experiment with you using different positions, sex toys, wigs, and costumes. But, remember: Action is his middle name, especially when it comes to sex. Unlike other GuyTypes, he's not particularly keen on talking, reading, or theorizing about sex. He doesn't need to find some deep philosophical meaning in sex; he just wants to enjoy it with you, in the maximum way possible—he is a "love doer." As part of a lovemaking date night, invite him to an adult shop where you can shop for lotions, lubricants, toys, costumes, and other sex goodies. Ask him for advice on picking out a special item for the night's intimacy activities. Then, when you get home, put your new purchase into play, and revel as your Excitement Seeker becomes a roaring sex machine (batteries not needed) who will fill you with more pleasure than you ever thought possible.

WHAT KIND OF A FATHER WILL HE BE?

The Excitement Seeker dad is like a big kid himself—playful, spontaneous, and fun. He will entertain, enthrall, and have a blast playing with your children—they will love him for it. He's the type of dad who will get down in the mud to play with the kids, engage in perpetual water fights, piggyback races, and childlike roleplay games—those squeals of delight during playtime may be coming from your children, or they may be coming from him. He will likely be the fun parent, so it's best if you can add a little strictness to counterbalance his easygoing parenting style. As a father, he will encourage your children to develop their independence, sense of adventure and fun, and optimistic approach to experiencing life. He's the perfect nonjudgmental dad who allows your children to develop their own identity while having fun and joy while doing it.

Here are some positives about the Excitement Seeker dad:

*He is highly entertaining.

*He can promote family activities.

*He can turn crisis into comedy.

*He is nonjudgmental about his children's friends.

*Children enjoy his company and seek him out.

WHAT KIND OF A HUSBAND WILL HE MAKE?

The Excitement Seeker is the type of husband who is fun-loving, spontaneous, and attuned to the pleasures of life. He will entertain you, surprise you, and romance you in his own action-oriented, "anything goes" style—as both of you savor the best that life has to offer. The more Introverted types (see Chapter 7) will stimulate your thrill-seeking, nature-loving side by taking you on nature outings, as well as outdoor adventures such as kayaking, white river rafting, bungee jumping, hunting, fishing, and the like. The more Extraverted types (see Chapter 7) will titillate you by inviting you to join them on exciting trips, social activities, and adventures that revolve around lights, action, fun, and people (the more, the merrier). You will rarely be bored with an Excitement Seeker; he is a wonderful and engaging companion who will always have a new adventure or surprise in store for you.

Another great thing about the Excitement Seeker guy is that he can accept negative comments about his habits—what other types would consider to be nagging and nitpicking—and it hardly bothers him.

Your Excitement Seeker guy also has the chameleon's ability to assume different characters and personas to please you. This can seem to be a great benefit, but also poses a challenge if he is not being himself in his attempt to please you. For example, he can appear to be more quiet and easygoing if he knows you're more of an Introvert (even though he may not be)—but he may not be able to keep up his character for long after you get married. It's not that he's trying to be fake—he may have good intentions in wanting to please you, and can be quite convincing in his behavior—but it won't last long, if he doesn't genuinely have some of that characteristic already in him (in this case, Introversion).

Although your Excitement Seeker may have a temper, he is like a tropical storm, in that his anger is likely to pass as quickly as it arises, and then he'll be ready to get back to the fun. Most of the time, he will tend to have an uncritical, happy disposition, and he will be accepting and tolerant about the marriage—realizing that nothing is perfect, but things can always get better.

One drawback to the Excitement Seeker husband may be his carefree attitude toward money. An Excitement Seeker has a tendency to splurge—he sees money as something to be used and enjoyed, not necessarily saved up. As a result, his generosity may be costly. He may buy you a mink coat on your birthday, even though you may need the money for other more practical reasons (who's paying the mortgage?). He delights in your (hopefully) surprised pleasant reactions when you open the expensive gift.

When it gets serious, and two Excitement Seekers fall in love and marry, the party is on. As a couple, you thrive on raw energy—you travel and party well together; you laugh well together. Of course, sometimes you may not work well together (housework, etc.) because you are easily distracted—you can always find something fun and interesting to do. You're always up to exploring something new—a new shop, museum, or restaurant—and you like to spend money and time on action-filled opportunities (trips and recreation).

As optimists, you look on the bright side of life—your mutual humorous touch and sense of irreverence (you don't take things too seriously) can keep your spirits up when life gets tough.

When it comes to the wedding, you may want to try something unconventional and original—getting married aboard a ship or hot air balloon—or a quickie wedding in Vegas. And, when it comes to the honeymoon, you may want one filled with action and adventure: parachuting, scuba diving, surfing, skiing, gambling, seeing shows, and taking excursions in remote areas.

On the downside, since both of you are natural flirts, there is a danger that one, or both of you, may fall into a sexual affair. Also, there is sometimes a tendency toward addiction in this type (seeking the next "high" or thrill), and an Excitement Seeking couple may unwittingly encourage each other's destructive habits.

But, despite the pitfalls, the good news is this: When two Excitement Seekers marry, they can sparkle and shine for everyone to see—like two playful puppies, they chase each other through life, oblivious to the rest of the world. Playful and fun, they know exactly how to have a good time and live a joy-filled life.

CHEATER'S ALERT

One of the challenges of being with an Excitement Seeker (especially an Extraverted one) is that he may have a tendency to cheat (or at least may appear as if he is). That doesn't mean that he will actually cheat on you, as long as the love, commitment, and trust is there. The issue with an Excitement Seeker (especially an Extraverted one) is that his charismatic and playful nature can come off as flirtatious—consequently, he can attract others easily, and he may be tempted to cheat. Also, being spontaneous, he may allow himself to get carried away with the moment and end up in a sexual situation he will later regret. The good news is that an Excitement Seeker can be faithful (and fantastic in bed with you) if the love is there.

WHAT ARE THE PROS AND CONS OF MARRYING THE EXCITEMENT SEEKER GUYTYPE?

PROS: He is fun-loving, spontaneous, and adventurous. He will get you to try things you never would have imagined doing on your own (hot air balloon rides, or maybe even some parachuting?). This guy is nonjudgmental; he embraces you as he finds you, and is among the most tolerant of the GuyTypes. With him as your ultimate "partner in fun," you will sample the greatest ecstasies the world has to offer—as you explore life together as one never-ending thrill ride.

CONS: The Excitement Seeker can be resistant to marriage or commitment (some may even tend toward being flirts and "lady's men," especially the more Extraverted types—see Chapter 7). It's not that he can't be faithful; it's just that he likes to maintain his freedom and flexibility. If you can give him a long enough "social leash" (he can talk, but he can't touch), then he will likely remain faithful and loyal to you in a long-term relationship.

OVERALL: You can't ask for a more fun and joyous companion in life. As your husband, he will motivate you to take risks, experiment, and become the best you can be—all the while encouraging you to experience life at its fullest. Exotic travelling, business opportunities, social alliances, exciting opportunities and experiences—he will place all of this and more at your feet. He can also be very romantic—even over the top—in his expressions of love for you. Excitement Seekers have been known to hire airplanes to send messages of love to their partner, and to cover themselves in chocolate and cherries as they jump out of a cake for their honey's birthday (he may also do a sexy dance for you—Magic Mike, sit down). Not only is he an accomplished lover and consummate companion, he can also get things done. He's a man of action who can be handy around the house with tools—fixing the washing machine and keeping the yard looking sharp, so you can focus on getting ready for your romantic evening together. Pop the champagne, turn up the volume, and get ready for the Big Show with your Excitement Seeker—let the good times roll.

Chapter 7:
The Twist of Introversion(I) / Extraversion(E): Why Your Guy's Social Energy Level Can Make a Big Difference

Here's a hint: All GuyTypes are <u>not</u> created equal.

There are the Introverted kind (also known as I), as well as the more Extraverted ones (known as E).

Introverted Guys are those who get more energy from their own thoughts, and like to be with a few friends in quieter places.

Extraverted Guys are those who get more energy from other people and thrive in outside environments with plenty of social interaction.

The term Introversion/Extraversion is referred to as the Energizing Dimension because it describes the way we get energy—either from our own thoughts (Introversion) or from other people in a social setting (Extraversion). The term was originally coined by the influential psychologist Carl Jung. Jung observed that some people were like turtles—they liked being in a comfortable shell of inner comfort, and they mainly acquired energy from their own thoughts. Other people, Jung observed, were like rabbits—they liked to interact a lot in the outside world, and gathered their energy from social interaction.

Introversion/Extraversion refer to the process of recharging our mental batteries—our bounce back time. Extraverts are "stimulus hungry"—they seek external stimulation and recharge their energy by social interaction. When an Extravert goes to a party, he usually likes to stay late and gets more energy as the night progresses.

The Introvert, on the other hand, recharges by withdrawing into their private comfort—staying home—listening to music, playing games on their tablet, reading on their phone, or just thinking. When they go to a party, they usually leave early, and then go home to recharge their energies.

Ask Yourself the "Fun Question" to Determine Your Social Energy Level

Are you an Introvert or an Extravert? You might say that you are both Introvert and Extravert, depending on the situation. Although you may engage in both Introverted and Extraverted activities, the key is where you get a majority of your energy—either internally from your own thoughts (Introvert energy source)—or externally by interacting with other people (Extravert energy source). Some Introverted people (entertainers, speakers, and teachers) can seem quite Extraverted for short periods of time, but then they need to go home to renew their energy (soaking in the hot tub), while Extraverts get more energy as the night progresses.

A quick way to determine if you're Introverted or Extraverted is to ask yourself the "Fun Question":

"What do you do for fun in your spare time?"

You are an Introvert (I), If you say, "I like to read, write, think, meditate, listen to music, and spend time with a companion or a few close friends."

You are an Extravert (E) if you say, "I like to hang out with friends," and you mention various sociable activities that you do on a weekly basis that involve other people (bowling, karaoke, shopping with girlfriends, etc.).

The key to this question is what you actually do on a daily or weekly basis, and how your activities determine your social energy.

Here are more characteristics of the Introvert and Extravert:

<u>If you're an Extravert:</u>

You describe yourself as happy when you're with others, having fun, and engaging in the outside world.

You may talk out loud—even when you're alone—because you like to experience an external event and make your thoughts real. You tend to act before reflecting.

As an Extravert, you require an outward goal to stay involved—you become restless below a certain level of external stimulation. You may feel depleted/overtaxed by the kind of inner mental activity that motivates and energizes the Introvert.

You also strive to broaden your sphere of influence—you want to affect circumstances in a way that is visible to others—you are affected by other's opinions and expectations.

Moreover, you need consistent contact with a face-to-face community in which others are invested and participate: family, workplace, faith community, voluntary organization, peer group, sports events, and fan clubs.

As an Extravert, you may recognize your Introvert side only when an external situation falls apart—when there is a crisis, divorce, loss of job, catastrophic illness, or death in the family.

When you are energized, you seek more stimulation: You talk to another person; you stop off at one more place; you sign another client.

You hunger for pace, variation, and expressive engagement. You're the type of person who expresses yourself freely, and you are comfortable initiating social encounters. You also want external space for events to occur. You relish the opportunity to express yourself—you may believe that thoughts aren't real until they are spoken aloud. You thrive on action, movement, and experiences that can be seen or heard.

To feel valued, you want to receive feedback about your performance—a return of energy to its source. You want to engage in social interaction to make your ideas more real—you want to make your thoughts come alive by exchanging them with others.

<u>If you're an Introvert:</u>

As an Introvert, you describe yourself as happiest when you're comfortable in your own skin, and have enough space and privacy to pursue your own path.

You like to consolidate your territory—you like your alone time and space. You don't share your inner world right away, and you may resist the influence of your partner when he tries to make you talk. For you, the inner world comes first. Of course, in our highly Extraverted world, this can be a challenge because the world urges you to socialize and speak up, even when you don't want to.

As an Introvert, you also have a lower threshold for social stimulation than an Extravert—you tend to be overwhelmed by too much external stimulation. After you've been at a party for a certain period of time, you've had enough, and you need to go home to recharge your battery (listen to music, think, read, or meditate).

When you withdraw from social interaction as an Introvert, it doesn't necessarily mean that you're shy. In my book, *The Gift of Shyness*, I talk about non-shy Introverts—they are comfortable socializing, but have a limited amount of energy to expend socially—when they're depleted, they need to go off by themselves to renew their energies.

Another characteristic of the Introvert is that you like to use as few words as possible to get the message across. For you, language is carefully and selectively used. That's why you can be puzzled and annoyed if your Extraverted partner overwhelms you with a lot of words and information that you weren't seeking or asking for (a confessional story even).

One thing to keep in mind is that type preferences can vary in intensity. Some people can be mildly Introverted (or Extraverted), while some can be very strong in this dimension. So, when you're evaluating yourself and others, it's good to keep in mind how strong the Introversion/Extraversion dimension is—mild or strong?

Here's a chart that summarizes the Extravert's/Introvert's differences:

E	I
Initiating	Receiving
Sociable/Active	Reserved/Contained
Friendly/like to join group activities	Likely have a few close friends / not likely to join social groups very often
Active	Reflective
Prefer to speak	Prefer to listen/communicate in writing
More likely the center of attention	More likely calm and enjoy solitude, seeking the background
Usually stay late at a social event and gets more energy as the night progresses	Usually go to a social event early and leave early
Can talk extensively and can keep going	Can talk extensively, but then gets tired and stops talking
Good talker	Good listener
Can be perfectly content with small talk	Likes to discuss deep topics
May get antsy if have to sit still too long without social interaction	Has patience for reading and introspective tasks like meditation
Likes crowds and sounds—the more, the better	Doesn't like loud social venues

HOW TO DO YOU EVALUATE A GUY'S NUMBER OF FACEBOOK FRIENDS?

If the guy you're interested in has more than 1000 friends on Facebook, then he has a greater probability of being an Extravert. The one exception is if he is Introverted, but uses his Facebook for a public or business capacity—he's a public speaker, politician, or marketer. In that case, he may have more than 1,000 friends, but could still be Introverted (you can look at other clues we've already mentioned). At the same time, you might find an Extravert who has a smaller number of friends, but is more selective in who he chooses as Facebook friends in his personal life—again, look at the other clues to determine if he is Introvert or Extravert.

Who is Better for You in a Romantic Relationship: An Introvert or Extravert?

The answer is that "It depends." Some research shows that Introverts get along best with each other, as do Extraverts with Extraverts. However, female Introverts can do well with male Extraverts (they balance each other out), while a non-traditional couple—female Extraverts with male Introverts—tend to do worse (in sex, chores, communication, and finances).

In reality, there are advantages to a couple being the same in this Energizing Dimension (both Introverts or both Extraverts) since they can enjoy the same social style. At the same time, there are some advantages to being different, since the Introvert can teach the Extravert how to relax and focus on their inner world, while the Extravert can help socialize the Introvert.

Therefore, instead of making a specific recommendation as to which type is best for you along the Introvert/Extravert dimension, we will examine what the Introvert/Extravert dimension looks like among the four different GuyTypes. Then, by observation and experimentation, you can determine whether you prefer an Extraverted or Introverted version of your ideal GuyType.

Choosing the Introverted or Extraverted GuyType

When you GuyType dates (determine their romantic style), it is helpful to ascertain their social energy level, i.e., their degree of Introversion/Extraversion, because it will tell you even more about their personality and character, as well as how compatible you will be with them (based on your own level of Introversion/Extraversion). For example, an Extraverted Excitement Seeker is the type of guy who is very charismatic and sociable, and is often seen at parties, concerts, clubs, and social get togethers. An Introverted Excitement Seeker, however, may be the strong, silent man of action who gets things done with his hands and his ingenuity—fixing things, enjoying outdoor activities, and living a life of freedom, independence, and adventure.

Just like you did when you scored yourself, you can determine a guy's social energy style (Introverted or Extraverted) by asking him the "Fun Question":

"What do you do for fun in your spare time?"

<u>He is likely an Introvert</u> if he likes to spend most of his time alone (at home) or with a few close friends.

<u>He is likely an Extravert</u> if he likes to spend most of his time socializing with people in the outside world.

Here are a few other clues you can look for:

INTROVERT	EXTRAVERT
Has a few Facebook friends	Has many Facebook friends
His Facebook shows relatively few social activities he's been involved in	His Facebook shows a large number of parties, people, and happening social events
He uses fewer words when he talks, but he makes an impact	He uses a lot of words when he talks
He doesn't tell long stories	He tells long stories
He likes to read, think, meditate, listen to music	He likes to hang out with friends and do things in fun social environments

To complete your GuyType mate selection puzzle, let's examine each of the four GuyTypes by adding the dimension of Introversion/Extraversion. Once you add the Introversion/Extraversion dimension, you will have a more in-depth picture of the type of guy you want to get involved with.

DATING THE INTROVERTED OR EXTROVERTED MEANING SEEKER

<u>If you're with an Introverted Meaning Seeker</u>, he is likely to be more low-key in the activities he enjoys with you (romantic comedy movie night at home or walks along a secluded beach). He may also be more spiritual, philosophical, and poetic than Extraverted Meaning Seekers. He also may not be as communicative (as often) as his Extraverted counterpart. Don't be fooled, however, some Introverted Meaning Seekers can talk a lot; but, they do so in short bursts—then

they need to recharge their batteries by going into their man cave to think, read, write, meditate, or listen to music.

Bottom Line: An Introverted Meaning seeker is the perfect guy for you if you like that wise, deep, loving kind of man who may speak less often, but when he does, he has something meaningful and profound to say.

If you're with an Extraverted Meaning Seeker, then get ready for conversation (and plenty of it), as well as social fun times with plenty of friends. Extraverted Meaning Seekers like to take you to self-help workshops, talks, and conferences, as well as art gallery openings, wine/cheese tastings, church and spiritual activities and events, concerts, and outdoor activities where plenty of people are present. They also enjoy networking with you at parties and social events. Since they are often excellent communicators, you will rarely be bored, and if you're shy or Introverted yourself, they can serve as your personal Icebreaker since they can start a conversation anywhere, anytime.

Bottom Line: An Extraverted Meaning Seeker guy is perfect for you if you want a sociable, communicative, and outgoing companion who shares his feelings and includes you in the social fun.

DATING THE INTROVERTED OR EXTROVERTED EXCITEMENT SEEKER

If you're with an Introverted Excitement Seeker, he is probably a hands-on type of man who is good with his hands (in more ways than one). He may be skilled at arts and crafts, mechanics, or sports activities. You can spend time with him playing pool, bowling, or taking a walk in nature. Although he may be communicative at times, he tends to be the strong, silent type who takes care of things that need to be taken care of (fixing the car; landscaping the yard), and then goes into his man cave to tinker with his hobbies and interests.

Bottom Line: An Introverted Excitement Seeker is the perfect guy for you if you want that strong, silent type—a "man's man" who gets things done—his word is his bond, and his actions speak louder than his words.

If you're with an Extraverted Excitement Seeker, then get ready for fun, people, and conversation. Extraverted Excitement Seekers like to take you to ball games, parties, concerts, casinos, networking events, car races, grand openings, and other social activities that are filled with action, friends, and fun. Since he is so skilled at interacting with, and charming people, you will always be immersed in a lively and fun social environment when you're with him.

Bottom Line: An Extraverted Excitement Seeker guy is perfect for you if you want a sociable, communicative, and outgoing companion who can break the ice easily and create excitement (and valuable business contacts and networking alliances) everywhere he goes.

DATING THE INTROVERTED OR EXTROVERTED KNOWLEDGE SEEKER

If you're with an Introverted Knowledge Seeker, he is likely the brainy, intellectual kind of guy who may love science, philosophy, and systems—he may even be the nerdy, absent-minded professor type who is caught up in his grand theories and ideas. With him, you can enjoy science fiction movie nights or playing intellectual games or puzzles online. He may also be more bookish and reclusive than Extraverted Knowledge Seekers. The interesting thing about him is that he can be quite talkative (for short bursts) when he's talking about one of his pet interests—abstract and theoretical topics like the possibility of intelligent life on other planets, or the existence of an afterlife.

Bottom Line: An Introverted Knowledge Seeker is the perfect guy for you if you like that smart, funny, and insightful kind of man who can stimulate your mind and make you realize that brains are definitely sexy.

If you're with an Extraverted Knowledge Seeker guy, then you are going to be around a very powerful and creative man. He is the type of innovator and mental leader who can come up with, and implement, great ideas to change the world. When you're with him, he's likely to take you to business and personal development workshops, talks, and conferences, as well as art gallery openings, wine/cheese tastings, and events, concerts, and other activities where something important can be learned, and something useful can be gained.

Bottom Line: An Extraverted Knowledge Seeker guy is perfect for you if you want a powerful, sociable, and innovative "mover and shaker," who makes his presence felt everywhere he goes—a scintillating companion who will expose you to new opportunities to learn and grow.

DATING THE INTROVERTED OR EXTRAVERTED SECURITY SEEKER

If you're with an Introverted Security Seeker, he is likely to be more low-key in the activities he enjoys with you (home cooked meals and Netflix). He is the perfect supporter, and even cheerleader, if you happen to be an ambitious person. He can be perfectly content being a stay-at-home dad while you conquer the business or work world. Just don't take his calm and helpful ways for granted. He is an exceptionally hard worker, and will sacrifice a lot for his family—all he needs is an occasional word of appreciation, and he's good to go.

Bottom Line: An Introverted Security Seeker is the perfect guy for you if you like that loyal, dedicated, and calm family kind of man who is always beside you, supporting you.

If you're with an Extraverted Security Seeker, then you will probably find yourself with a very sociable man who is also a leader. This is a traditional, strong kind of man who likes to take charge of his relationships, work, and life (and he is usually pretty good at it). Get ready to socialize a lot with this guy in formal functions: Black Tie dinners, charity events, and the like. He likes to get out on the town and make his presence felt, and he probably has a good number of friends, fans, and supporters who are likely to be by his side.

<u>Bottom Line</u>: An Extraverted Security Seeker guy is perfect for you if you want a strong, sociable leader type of man who will take care of you, protect you, and love you the old-fashioned way.

Introvert or Extravert: Choose Your Favorite GuyType Version

Now that you know what your GuyType looks like as an Introvert or Extravert, you can determine which version works best for you in a long-term relationship. You might want to experiment by dating both an Introvert and Extravert version of your ideal GuyType, and see which one fits better with you. You may find that you like the Introvert one better (or maybe the Extravert one). Once you do your dating homework, you will have more information at your disposal to base your romantic decisions—you'll be better able to pinpoint exactly the type of guy you're most likely to enjoy being with in a long-term relationship.

Chapter 8:
Personality Networking:
How to GuyType Your Dates and
Find Mr. Right

You're about to learn a new and fun way to meet guys and find the right one for you. It's called Personality Networking, or GuyTyping, based on a unique combination of social networking and psychological profiling. In this approach, instead of dating blindly hoping to find Mr. Right, you will systematically interact with men based on their personality compatibility. You will quickly determine a date's love personality style, or GuyType, and recognize if he's compatible with you for a long-term relationship. Then, you will learn how to break the ice and develop rapport based on your understanding of his GuyType, or romantic style.

It's fun and easy.

Here are some approaches you can use:

JOIN THE RIGHT PERSONALITY
NETWORK

One efficient way to meet your ideal GuyType is to join the right Personality Network—organizations and networks (both online and off) that are geared to your most compatible GuyType. If, for example, you are an Excitement Seeker, and your ideal match is the Excitement Seeker, you will join a Network/Community that is geared to Excitement Seekers (action-oriented, social, and fun).

When you join a Personality Network, you maximize your dating time because you're in the right environment to meet the exact personality type you're looking for—you have a larger pool of the right kind of GuyType for you (whether it's the Excitement Seeker, Meaning Seeker, and so on).

See Chapters 3 through 6 on each of the four GuyTypes for tips on the types of organizations and groups where you're likely to encounter the guy you're looking for. You can also check out the Appendix which contains a list of online organizations and communities (most of which also have an offline presence) where you are most likely to meet your compatible GuyType.

Remember that you are generally looking for a GuyType who matches your LoveTemperament (If you're a Security Seeker, your best match is likely a Security Seeker, and so forth). Here are a few ideas of where to find your ideal GuyType:

If he's a Meaning Seeker, you can find him at organizations that involve psychology, philosophy, the arts, spirituality, and humanitarian causes (See Chapter 3 and the Appendix).

If he's a Knowledge Seeker, you can find him at organizations related to entrepreneurship, innovation, science, politics, finance, and wealthy or upscale lifestyles. (See Chapter 4 and the Appendix).

If he's a Security Seeker, you can find him at organizations that cater to family, the home, community, country, animals, children, and traditional customs and traditions. (See Chapter 5 and the Appendix).

If he's an Excitement Seeker, you can find him at organizations related to outdoor activities, sports or extreme sports, traveling, fine dining, wine tasting, entertainment, music, comedy dancing, and socializing. (See Chapter 6 and the Appendix).

Once you're participating in the type of Personality Network your guy is likely to be involved with, you have a higher probability of meeting your ideal GuyType there. You will find it much easier to find a compatible man who also meets your requirements for physical attractiveness, religion, education, hobbies, personal interests, and other important factors. In addition, you will have an easier time breaking the ice, and getting to know him, because you have more in common. You can confirm his GuyType by using GuyType Profiling: Asking the 3 Magic Questions or making the GuyType Micro-Observations below.

USE GUYTYPE PROFILING TO "CATCH" MR. RIGHT

In common parlance, profiling refers to an analysis of psychological and behavioral characteristics to identify a particular subgroup of people. It is used in law enforcement to apprehend criminals who behave in certain patterns.

In your case, you will use profiling to "catch," (i.e., identify and meet) your ideal mate for a long-term relationship. You will do so through "micro-interactions"—asking a few simple questions and making a few basic observations (micro-observations), both online and off, in the course of your daily activities. The beauty of the GuyType approach is that you can ask one question at a time (or analyze his online and offline behavior) in an efficient way that gives you a lot of information about his GuyType (romantic personality style), so you can make a connection and develop a quality relationship with him. In our time-crunched mobile society, the GuyTypes dating approach can fit in perfectly with your busy lifestyle.

There are two components to GuyType Profiling your prospective matches: Asking the 3 Magic Questions and making the micro-observations, as follows:

ASK THE 3 MAGIC QUESTIONS

The first approach to GuyTyping that handsome guy (determining his romantic style) is by asking him the 3 Magic Questions from Chapter 2. You can do this both online (dating sites, dating apps) and off. You can ask the questions in person, by email, text, Facebook, or Twitter (or other social media vehicles).

Whenever you run into an attractive guy you would like to GuyType (to determine compatibility), ask the questions below during the course of normal conversation. The good thing about these questions is that they are common, unobtrusive questions that often come up in conversation. As a result, he won't think that you are trying to "analyze" him, which is something that turns some people off. You will ask the normal type of questions that people use when they want to get to know someone.

You can also experiment with asking your own version of a particular question (that taps into one of the personality dimensions). For example, instead of asking him if he would go to Vegas spontaneously ("The Vegas Question"), you can ask him if he likes to do things spontaneously (then, to verify: On another occasion, ask him to meet you somewhere spontaneously, and see how he reacts).

Or, you can even make statements that invite him to respond. For example, instead of asking what his favorite movie is, you can start talking about your favorite movies, and then see if he volunteers his own favorites.

Here are the three questions to determine his GuyType:

Question 1: What would you do if you won $10 million? If he uses the money for some innovative or creative purpose (start a revolutionary eco-business to save the planet), he is probably the Intuitive (give him N for Intuitive). If he would use it for reasons related to practicality (save and invest) or sensory experiences (enjoy it for pleasurable activities like fine dining and traveling), then he is likely the Sensor (give him the letter S, for Sensor).

Question 2: What's your favorite movie and why do you like it? If he liked the movie because of the way it made him feel (the relationships, inspiring aspects, maybe he felt like crying, or did), then he is likely the Feeler (give him the letter "F" for Feeling). If he liked the movie because of the way it made him think (the plot, direction, special effects), he is a Thinker (give him the letter "T" for Thinking).

Question 3: Your friend invites you to Vegas (or a luxury resort—name one), the next day (a work or school day), would you go? If he says, "Yes," then he is a <u>Perceiver</u> (spontaneous; give him the letter "P" for spontaneous). If he says, "No," or "I have to plan it out," he is the Judger (structured; give him the letter "J" for <u>Judger</u>—he is structured and schedule-oriented like a Judge).

Now, write down the letters that represent his answers:

_____   _____   _____

For example, he may have scored something like:

<u>S</u> (Sensor)   <u>F</u> (Feeler)   <u>J</u> (Judger or structured)

Out of his 3 letters (responses), you will only choose 2 of them to make up his GuyType based on the 4 GuyTypes below.

In the case above, he would be an:

<u>S</u>   <u>J</u>   (Security Seeker)

Now, as for the prospective date you're GuyTyping, check below to see which of the two-letter combinations he falls into:

Summary:

If he has the letter N and F, then he is the **Meaning Seeker** (see Chapter 3).

If he has the letter N and T, then he is the **Knowledge Seeker** (see Chapter 4).

If he has the letter S and J, then he is the **Security Seeker** (see Chapter 5).

If he has the letter S and P, then he is the **Excitement Seeker** (see Chapter 6).

When you GuyType your dates, remember that psychological preferences may vary in strength. One guy, for example, may appear strong on N (Intuitive), but mild on F (Feeler). Thus, although he's an NF overall (Meaning Seeker), he may not be a particularly strong one (some of the characteristics of the NF may not apply to him, while others will). Or, you might meet another guy who is strong in both N and F, and you can determine that he is a strong NF (Meaning Seeker)—he has a majority of the Meaning Seeking characteristics.

Another factor to consider is that a guy may have both a primary, or main GuyType, as well as a secondary one (less preferred but still in use). For example, his primary GuyType may be NF (Meaning Seeker), while his secondary is NT (Knowledge Seeker). Thus, for the most part, he will be searching for meaning and intimacy (NF), and the rest of the time he will be focused on attaining knowledge and competence (NT).

Here's something important to keep in mind as you begin to GuyType the men you meet: Not all GuyTypes are created the same. Your goal is to become a smart GuyType profiler who looks at all the clues a guy is giving you, so you can make the right determination as to what his true GuyType is, and whether he's compatible with you for a long-term relationship.

MAKE MICRO-OBSERVATIONS

If you don't like asking questions (you think they may be intrusive or pushy), another approach is to profile him into a certain GuyType category by making micro-observations (reading the verbal and nonverbal cues) that reveal his true personality style.

Here's what to look for, depending on the guy you're looking for.

How to GuyType The Meaning Seeker (NF)

Since he lives in the world of imagination and feeling, he may be less physically graceful or skilled with mechanical things. Introverted Meaning Seekers, especially, can even be awkward—due to their lack of attention to the physical world around them. Since they have their mind on higher things, they may not notice the edge of a table or the beginning of a flight of stairs—consequently, they may stumble or appear clumsy.

In general, Meaning Seekers tend to talk in metaphors, abstractions, and similes. They like humor that has a message or meaning to it.

In terms of fashion, the Meaning Seekers (especially the Extraverted ones) tend to be innovative trendsetters who create a unique look. They like soft lines and colors.

His Fashion Motto: "Make a unique statement with flair—a personalized look."

Nonverbal Clues:
In terms of his nonverbal communication, he may extend his open hand to others, as if offering his counsel freely or accepting another's words as a gift. He may bring his hands together in various ways, as if trying to hold together two halves of a message.

Here are more clues:

*He likes to use emoticons.

*He may have an artistic and ethereal (otherworldly) quality about him—detached from material quests and focused on spiritual things (or things that affect humanity).

*When speaking, he has a certain warmth and personal tone to his voice. He tends to lean in, look people closely in the eye, and respond with gestures of empathy and concern.

*He is genuinely concerned about other people, including strangers. He may ask the waitress what her goals in life are, even though he doesn't know her.

*He is empathetic. He seems to know how you're feeling and cares about your mood.

*He can wax poetic on many topics, including psychology, philosophy, spirituality (self-actualization), and the arts.

*He likes to talk about missions, values, passions, and purpose.

*He loves to use the word "Love" a lot, as in "I love this," and so forth.

*He may like romantic comedies, or heart-warming types of movies, because of the relationships and the way he felt after watching them.

*He doesn't talk a lot about what he observes—instead, he tends to make intuitive leaps (he may also exaggerate).

*He tends to be an "incurable romantic," enjoying giving and receiving romantic gestures (cards, poetry, gifts, words of endearment).

How to GuyType The Knowledge Seeker (NT)

Knowledge Seekers come in two varieties: Introverts (they prefer to get energy from their own thoughts and tend to have a few close friends) and Extraverts (they prefer to get energy by socializing with others in the outside world). See Chapter 7 for more details on the differences between the Introverted and the Extraverted Knowledge Seeker.

Extraverted Knowledge Seekers tend to focus on external manifestations of power and success. They may demonstrate their status and influence by wearing designer clothing, driving luxury or exotic cars, surrounding themselves with important people, owning lavish homes, and belonging to exclusive clubs or organizations.

Introverted Knowledge Seekers, on the other hand, like to demonstrate their intellectual power and knowledge through their work, as well as by using their witty, sarcastic, and incisive use of words. They may not care much about external manifestations of luxury or success. They may even have an unconventional or rumpled look—kind of like the brilliant, absent-minded genius.

Overall, Knowledge Seekers choose clothes for comfort and utility. They don't pay much attention to conventional practices; they also consider price and durability—they may keep clothes for years, especially the more frugally-minded Introverted Knowledge Seekers.

Moreover, Knowledge Seekers appear to have powerful personas—they like to get to the point and can appear quite blunt and controlling at times.

In addition, they are fascinated about ideas, and can talk for quite a bit of time about remote and unusual things that they are interested in (although other people may not know what they're talking about).

His Fashion Motto:

For Extraverted Knowledge Seekers: "Clothes demonstrate status."

For Introverted Knowledge Seekers: "Clothes are not a high priority, except as required by my job."

Nonverbal Clues:
In terms of nonverbal gestures, he may use hand gestures to express the need for precision and control. He may make one or both hands into claws as if to seize the idea he is discussing. He may use his finger like a calculator—ticking off point after point.

Here are more clues:

*He is sarcastic and witty in his texts and emails.

*He likes science, technology, business, and innovation.

*He judges people based on their competence and ability.

*He likes puzzle-like movies that stimulate his mind and imagination: mysteries, thrillers, sci-fi.

*He may be tight with money, or as he would call it, "A good saver."

*He is able to find the flaw in anything—he would make a great movie or restaurant critic. He wants to improve things and make them better.

*He can be blunt at times.

*He likes debate, argument, and even conflict (as long as it doesn't get personal) so he can stretch his intellectual muscles.

*He is competitive.

*He exudes confidence and competence (and wants others to be as equally competent).

How to GuyType the Security Seeker (SJ)

He is a family-oriented guy who may talk about his family a lot—often with pride, and also with a bit of criticism.

He likes talking about practical, everyday things such as sports, business, politics, home improvement, diet, and so forth (he's not necessarily the type to speak for hours on arcane topics like auras and universal energy).

Some people may call him boring and a stick-in-the-mud; he would refer to himself as conventional and appropriate.

When it comes to his appearance, you will find that he has a more conservative and appropriate style: Long-sleeve shirts and ties, suits, well-pressed clothes; well put-together accessories.

Overall, he prefers a classic look, and the takes methodical care of his clothing. He likes to adhere to a prescribed color plan.

His Fashion Motto: "Want a classic, long-lasting look."

Nonverbal Clues:
In terms of nonverbal gestures, he is likely to avoid showy hand gestures when he speaks; he may bring one or both hands in chopping

motions to emphasize his statements or to cut off further discussion. He tends to have good posture, sitting and standing up straight. He may walk deliberately, and at a fast pace—giving off the impression that he has somewhere important to go.

Here are some more clues:

*His texts and emails have a definite purpose and quickly get to the point.

*He is not a big risk taker; if you suggest a new activity, he may not sound too enthusiastic about it at first.

*He gets bored by esoteric and far-fetched ideas—he likes practical, down-to-earth conversations (I'm going to the barbershop today and getting a Hi-top fade; my new tax accountant can save me 10% this year).

*He is good at saving money and investing.

*He is family-oriented—you see plenty of family pictures on his Facebook, phone, and social media.

*He is more impressed by practicality and safety than "pie in the sky" ideas.

*He likes to stick to his routines—you're likely to see him regularly at Starbucks at 8am, and in the gym at 9am, Monday, Wednesday, and Friday.

*He likes to use his favorite phrases or pet names on a repetitive basis: "What's going on?" or "Honey-pie."

*He is a hard worker—often arriving early and working late at the office.

*He is the responsible one out of the group—the designated driver, the guy to cool down an altercation between his buddies.

How to GuyType the Excitement Seeker (SP)

On a date, he doesn't like to sit and talk about abstract or philosophical things (like Meaning Seekers)—he likes to talk about current events and practical things. Better yet, rather than talking, he likes to go out and do active things, like playing a game, or doing some outdoor activity (fishing, white river rafting).

He changes subjects frequently, and is prone to changing his mind on various topics. He may appear to be disorganized, but he would say that he knows where everything is—he has his own organizational style.

When it comes to clothing, he is likely to wear comfortable sporty clothes and accessories. He may prefer a sports coat instead of a suit; a sweat suit instead of pants or a suit. He is also aware of the look, texture, and color of his clothes, and he likes to look good.

Overall, he chooses clothes for impact—he prefers action-oriented garments that allow flexibility of movement. He chooses brands and labels that others will recognize. He can be bold, dashing, and daring in his style. He can artfully intertwine bargains with designer labels.

His Fashion Motto: "Make an impact on others."

Nonverbal Clues:
In terms of nonverbal gestures, he likes to smile (and laugh) a lot, and he tends to move gracefully, with the fluidity of an athlete. He is supremely comfortable in his own body and has great body awareness. He can make even the smallest action (pouring tea) into an art form—he makes physical tasks look easy.

Here are some more clues:

*His texts and emails are free-flowing and can ramble quickly from one topic to the next.

*You may see him doing outrageous things on social media—dancing on a table, eating the worm in a tequila bottle, kissing two women at once.

*He can be a smooth and charming talker and texter—wooing you with compliments and endearments.

*He's good at fixing things and he's good with his hands (let your imagination go on that one).

*He makes spur of the moment invitations to friends—"Let's go to Cancun tomorrow."

*He can be late, but has his own way of looking at time: free-flowing and spontaneous.

*He may post a bunch of different random things on his social media, which may include adventures, social events, or wild activities he's engaged in.

*He's all about fun and enjoying life.

*He can change plans on you suddenly—cancelling, but then making it up to you, in the extravagant way that only he can.

*He can make you laugh even when you're super mad at him.

*He's skilled at dealing with emergencies—he flies by the seat of his pants and often ends up in a winning position.

CATCHING YOUR GUY'S EYE ONLINE: HOW TO ATTRACT HIS INTEREST AND START A CONVERSATION

In our mobile technology world, it's never been easier to break the ice and get to know a prospective romantic partner:

Here's a few tips for you to meet your ideal Guy in our digital world:

Make Sure Your Facebook Profile Reflects Who You Really Are

To attract the right GuyType (someone similar to you), you need to make sure that you're displaying your authentic self (your true LoveTemperament) on Facebook and other social media. If, for example, you're an Excitement Seeker, do you have pictures posted of your outdoor adventures or fun social life? Maybe, you're shy or reluctant to post them; but, if these activities reflect the real you, it's important that you express who you are to a guy who could be your type (an Excitement Seeker, also), but may not know it, because you don't show your true colors. Remember: Guys will be checking out your profile (as you check out theirs), so you want to make sure that you represent your absolute true LoveTemperament (one that ideally matches with your most compatible GuyType).

Check your Facebook (and other social media) to see that you are consistent with your LoveTemperament, so you can attract the right GuyType:

If you're a Meaning Seeker: Post items related to your interests in psychology, philosophy, spirituality, and finding the meaning in life.

If you're a Knowledge Seeker: Post items related to your interests in science, technology, politics, law, religion, philosophy, esoterica, business, and new innovations.

If you're a Security Seeker: Post items related to your interests in saving, investing, home improvement, everyday events and news, vacations, sensual experiences (traveling, massages, hot tubbing, fine dining, and wine tasting), material acquisitions (cars, boats, property, latest technological gadgets), and things related to family (children), home, and country.

If you're an Excitement Seeker: Post items related to your interests in action-oriented activities (kayaking, boating, surfing, skiing, hunting, off-roading), as well as social fun, (parties, concerts, comedy clubs, resorts, dance clubs, charity events, live music, theatre).

Connect With Your Ideal Guy Through Your Online Friendship Base

You can use various social media platforms (Facebook, Twitter, Instagram, LinkedIn) to meet and connect with your ideal GuyType.

One approach is to get involved in Facebook Groups or Events (you can host, volunteer, or attend) that target a particular GuyType. For example, you can get involved in Facebook events and groups related to psychology (Meaning Seekers), technology (Knowledge Seekers), outdoor activities and social fun (Excitement Seekers), or family/tradition (Security Seekers).

You can also be on the lookout for cute guys (Facebook friends) who post or comment on topics that may give a clue as to their GuyType (technology and science for Knowledge Seekers, for example). Then, you can like, comment on, or share their posts—you can also send them a private message that you'd be interested in coffee to discuss the topic further.

Utilize Meetup Groups to Find Mr. Right

Meetup groups are another good way to target the ideal GuyType you're looking for. You can start, or join, a Meetup group in your area related to the topic that your ideal GuyType is interested in (e.g., family and community for a Security Seeker). You can also message members of the group, and go to in-person events and mixers. There are many groups that cater to the four GuyTypes. So, it is a good, low cost way to do your personality networking, and find the GuyType who best matches your romantic type.

Engage an Affinity Wing to Help You Find Your Ideal GuyType

An Affinity Wing is someone who can help you find your ideal GuyType online (and off) by personality networking on your behalf and making introductions. On Facebook, your friend can go to

"Suggest Friends" and introduce you to a compatible GuyType you're interested in.

Both online and off, an Affinity Wing can save you a lot of time (and help you out if you're shy) by breaking the ice and making the initial connection for you. If you don't have an outgoing friend who can help you, you might consider hiring someone to be your Affinity Wing. That person can join groups for you—online and off—to help you meet your ideal GuyType. They will go to events, make initial connections, and then introduce them to you. You can either accompany them on these outings (and they serve as a traditional wing person), or they can go solo, and then introduce you to the guys later (They tell the guy, "I've got a great person for you to meet").

If, for example, you're looking for a Security Seeker GuyType, these Affinity Wings can join Security Seeker organizations for you, mingle in Security Seeker hangouts, and introduce you to potential soul mate candidates as a desirable, possible match. In the singles world, Dating Wings are people who help shy or Introverted singles break the ice and meet someone by making the introductions. An Affinity Wing goes farther by specifically targeting guys who fit within your Personality Network, and who have an affinity for your romantic type. Once you are introduced to viable dating candidates, you can further screen them by using the tools you are learning in *GuyTypes*.

Use Memes as a Fun Way to GuyType Him

Instead of asking questions verbally to GuyType an attractive man, you can use memes (i.e., representative pictures or symbols that are spread on the Internet) to determine his GuyType. If, for example, you want to find out if he is a Thinker or a Feeler, you can message him a meme of a brain (head) and a heart (feelings), with the phrase: "If you had to, which would you choose?" Or, for the "Vegas" (spontaneity) question, you can send him a picture of a "work desk," and one with "Vegas at night," and ask, "You've got a free ticket, but you have to go tomorrow. Yes or no?"

Using memes can be a fun way to GuyType him (by getting his answers to the Magic Questions) without him even realizing that you're doing it.

Get Ready to Have Fun GuyTyping
the Men You Meet

Yes, GuyTyping can be a lot of fun. Think of yourself as a love detective; except instead of catching a bad man, you want to attract a good one. The GuyType method you choose will depend on your type and preference. If you're a social or group person, then joining an online or offline Personality Network and making new friends (including your potential soul mate) will be ideal for you. If you're more of a shy and Introverted person, then you may want to skip the whole Network (group) thing, and just GuyType dates on your own by using the 3 Magic Questions and micro-observations. And, if you just plain don't want to deal with the whole dating game, you can hire an Affinity Wing to do the heavy work for you, and you just follow up on the dates (ideally, you want your Affinity Wing to GuyType the men for you, so you know if they're compatible with you from the beginning).

Whichever method you choose, realize that you now have the control over your love life in your hands. Rather than waiting around for men to approach you (often incompatible ones), you can control the dating game and dramatically increase your odds of finding Mr. Right by following your GuyType game plan. Ask the right questions, make the necessary observations, and join the right networks, and you are well on your way to finding a compatible guy to share your life with.

Chapter 9:
How to Date Outside Your GuyType and Live Happily Ever After

Here's a dilemma: What if you're interested (or in love) with an amazing guy who happens to be a different type than you are? Let's say you're an Excitement Seeker, and you've fallen for that brainy, nerdy Knowledge Seeker.

What do you do now? Should you just discard that hot and wonderful man, or can you somehow create a lasting relationship with him?

Research shows that people who share similarities (in core values and personality traits) seem to attract each other, and they also tend to have more satisfying long-term relationships. On the other hand, you don't have to be exactly the same as your mate. A few surface differences (you like MMA; he likes tennis) can be fine because they can actually add a little spice and potential for growth in your relationship.

The key is to know what to expect when you date outside of your recommended GuyType pairing—when you date someone who is different, or even opposite from you (e.g., an Excitement Seeker with a Security Seeker). When you date someone who is quite different from you in key personality areas, you will probably have to work harder to accentuate the strength of the pairing, while minimizing any weaknesses.

The bottom line is that, "Yes, you can be happy with a GuyType who is different from your Type, IF…" you learn how to appreciate and respect the different type of guy that you're with. Here's some inside information about nonmatching pairings that can work if you put in some extra effort, and if you have enough in common to make it worth your while.

Meaning Seeker Combinations
Meaning Seeker (NF) with an Excitement
Seeker (SP)

The big difference here is what they value: Meaning (Meaning Seeker) versus Fun (Excitement Seeker). The good part is that the Excitement Seeker lightens the heart of the Meaning Seeker, while the Meaning Seeker enriches the heart of the Excitement Seeker. They can definitely make a passionate team with a positive bond of playful creativity and committed caring.

The Excitement Seeker admires the Meaning Seeker's good-heartedness, win-win attitude, and focus on harmony and consensus. And, the Meaning Seeker appreciates the Excitement Seeker's sexual appetite and fun-loving, mischievous nature (it's a nice release from the Meaning Seeker's sometimes overconsuming seriousness about life).

Although they can contribute positive things to each other, there are some areas that are different and can cause disharmony.

First of all, Meaning Seekers like to delve deeply into the relationship (with introspection and feeling), while Excitement Seekers can easily get bored or annoyed when the Meaning Seeker asks them for the umpteenth time, "How do you feel?" "What is the real meaning of this?" Consequently, Meaning Seekers can accuse Excitement seekers of being superficial, while Excitement Seekers will tell Meaning Seekers to, "get over it."

Although the Meaning Seeker goes to great lengths to please his mate, Excitement Seekers don't always appreciate their nurturing ways. To the carefree and tough-minded Excitement Seeker, the Meaning Seeker's compassion can be misconstrued as indecisive, spineless, and weak. Then, the Meaning Seeker may wonder why their mate is insensitive and incapable of understanding the nuances of their partnership (the Excitement Seeker quickly forgets quarrels, while the Meaning Seeker remembers them well).

On a positive note, this couple can get along well since the Meaning Seeker has a deep need for harmony, while the Excitement Seeker can be tolerant and flexible. Both can overlook hardships and persevere. Moreover, the decisive Excitement Seeker can help the indecisive Meaning Seeker. And the compassionate Meaning Seeker can help the fickle Excitement Seeker love unconditionally.

Overall, the good news is that when they can find a mutually satisfying emotional level, no other combo matches their dynamic relationship: funny, casual, sincere, accepting, endearing, and vibrant in their connection.

Here's a chart that summarizes the main differences:

MEANING SEEKER	EXCITEMENT SEEKER
Intimacy	Fun
Appreciation/Understanding	Praise
High Complexity	Low Complexity
Purposeful/Serious	Playful/Lighthearted
Strong Perfectionism	Scattered Productivity
Intense	Carefree
Depth, sincerity, compassion	Excitement, Warmth
Work, then play	Play, then work

Meaning Seeker (NF) with Knowledge Seeker (NT)

This couple makes for an interesting combination that can get along rather well, assuming they can understand and appreciate each other's style. The Meaning Seeker and Knowledge Seeker dislike wasting time on irrelevant and superficial conversations. Both have a strong interest in the abstract and internal world—ideas, concepts, principles, philosophies, and theories.

They also have complementary social skills: The Meaning Seeker is the most compassionate (eager to please and emotionally expressive), while the Knowledge Seeker can be blunt and ul-tra-competitive, but also can communicate with refreshing candor. As a result, the Meaning Seeker can soften up the Knowledge Seek-er's direct comments, while the Knowledge Seeker can help the Meaning Seeker speak their mind in social situations (say "NO" if you mean it).

Knowledge Seekers like the Meaning Seeker's enthusiasm, warmth, and insight into people. And, the Meaning Seeker appreciates the Knowledge Seeker's ambition and ability to concentrate and reach their goals.

Sometimes, however, the Knowledge Seeker is so focused on work that they may miss life's pleasures (their child's school activity) un-less their Meaning Seeker mate reminds them. The Meaning Seeker influences the Knowledge Seeker in a diplomatic way, and the pow-erful Knowledge Seeker respects a mate (the charming and deter-mined Meaning Seeker) who has the strength of character to stand up to their formidable personality.

The Meaning Seeker needs the Knowledge Seeker to teach them as-sertiveness, honest feedback, and to give them specific direction—to get the job done. Likewise, the Knowledge Seeker needs the Meaning Seeker to teach them compassion, soften their communication, and encourage them. The Meaning Seeker brings personal warmth to relationships—a quality that greatly appeals to the analytical, self-controlled Knowledge Seeker.

One challenge with this pairing is that Meaning Seekers don't like conflict, while Knowledge Seekers love a good debate over the fine points of definitions and logical categories. Meaning Seekers can indulge their Knowledge Seeker in spirited discus-sions for short periods of time; but, if it goes on too long, they can get bored, or worse yet, take it personally and feel hurt (they may ask, "Why are you always so sarcastic?"—sarcasm can hurt the Meaning Seeker).

The Knowledge Seeker says: "Do what I say, and we'll get along just fine."

The Meaning Seeker says: "Tell me you appreciate me, and I'll walk to the ends of the earth for you."

Here's a chart that summarizes their main differences:

MEANING SEEKER	KNOWLEDGE SEEKER
Biggest fear is disharmony	Biggest fear is being found incompetent
I want to feel close	You can't trust everyone
Emotional	Logical
Strong Perfectionism	High Productivity: If it's a job worth doing
Long-suffering	Impatient
Searches for Meaning	Searches for Knowledge
Loves deeply and is disappointed by those who can't love	Doesn't love easily, but can love deeply when they let themselves go

Knowledge Seeker Combinations
Knowledge Seeker (NT) with Excitement Seeker (SP)

Excitement Seekers are similar to Knowledge Seekers in that they both have a lack of possessiveness and reluctance to interfere with their mates—both have a freedom-loving nature. They also share a desire to ignore social convention and to obtain results in the most expedient way possible.

The Excitement Seeker has broader interests, while the Knowledge Seekers knows more about fewer topics. The Excitement Seeker respects the Knowledge Seeker's analytical, logical, and rational mind. The Knowledge Seeker admires the Excitement Seeker's curiosity, originality, and breadth of knowledge.

The Excitement Seeker likes the Knowledge Seeker's candor (they find it refreshing), while the Knowledge Seeker is charmed by the Excitement Seeker's free and easy way with people (it's sometimes difficult for the Knowledge Seeker to be accommodating to people since they like to be in charge).

From their perspective, Knowledge Seekers admire the Excitement Seeker's interest in tools and their hands-on skills—they also enjoy the Excitement Seeker's sense of fun, improvisation, and spontaneity (yes, even mischief). However, at times, the Excitement Seeker's fun and games may seem excessive and frivolous to the deep-thinking Knowledge Seekers.

Knowledge Seekers need Excitement Seekers because they can teach them charisma, will accept their leadership, and can cheerlead for them and their grand ideas and adventures. At the same time, Excitement Seekers will bring much needed fun and spontaneity to lighten up the Knowledge Seeker's intense way of looking at things.

On the other hand, Excitement Seekers need Knowledge Seekers to focus them and keep them on task. Excitement Seekers also need Knowledge Seekers for their ability to stimulate their imagination and think about the possibilities of the future—how to advance in their career and utilize their unique talents.

The truth is that Knowledge Seekers enjoy control, and they find no personality more impossible to control than Excitement Seekers. Like a bird, Excitement Seekers like to take off and land whenever they feel like it. This behavior can exasperate the Knowledge Seeker. Knowledge Seekers can also become upset with the Excitement Seeker's casual concern about financial matters, social obligation, and protocol. When it comes to social events, Excitement Seekers are often more interested in spending time with interesting people who like to laugh and enjoy life, rather than going to the Knowledge Seeker's stuffy parties with intellectual or self-important individuals.

Additionally, the Excitement Seeker can disappoint the Knowledge Seeker by their lack of interest in the internal world—Knowledge Seekers enjoy discussing theories, hypotheses, and the latest inventions and developments in the world. Breakfast with a Knowledge Seeker can easily turn into a long-drawn out, highly detailed lecture on some esoteric topic—quickly boring the Excitement Seeker.

Here's a chart that summarizes their main differences:

KNOWLEDGE SEEKER	EXCITEMENT SEEKER
Likes to be respected	Likes to be praised
Looks out for themselves	Hopes others will look out for them
Controlling	Craves freedom
Offers wisdom	Offers intrigue
Strategic	Carefree
Narrow Interests	Broad Interests
Work-oriented	Playful

Knowledge Seeker (NT) with Security Seeker (SJ)

The Security Seeker offers an invaluable gift to the Knowledge Seeker: a stable and reliable home center. Since Knowledge Seekers are often in their abstract clouds of thought, they may lose touch with the everyday workings of family life. When that happens, the Security Seeker steps in to see that things get done, especially the details of running a house.

Moreover, the Security Seeker can be comfortable with the Knowledge Seeker's skeptical attitude about people and life, and their obsession with their work. This attitude can resonate with the Security Seeker's sense of realistic pessimism (seeing things the way they are—not always pretty) and sense of duty ("Someone has to do it; it's usually me").

Although the Security Seeker may admire the Knowledge Seeker's intellect and ingenuity, they may feel left out of the Knowledge Seeker's highbrow intellectual life (and they can be bothered by the disdain that Knowledge Seekers have for "Plebeian" activities—everyday matters such as household chores).

Security Seekers also make sure that Knowledge Seekers have a social life—both share a strong loyalty to close friends and family; consequently, it's the Security Seekers who serves to remind the Knowledge Seeker about social functions and family traditions (a nephew's Bar Mitzvah; the niece's Quinceañera) that they would likely forget otherwise.

However, if the Security Seeker pushes too far, the Knowledge Seeker may feel nagged, and will try to protect their autonomy from the Security Seeker's bossiness.

In addition, Security Seekers like that Knowledge Seekers are bold in making decisions, while the Security Seeker's relaxed charm can calm the Knowledge Seeker. However, the one area they can butt heads is that Security Seekers respect authority and pride themselves on following social rules, while Knowledge Seekers refuse to obey conventions unless it suits their needs.

In terms of conversation, the Security Seeker finds it relaxing to exchange unrelated facts and trivia about the weather, entertainment, news, sports, and people—the type of chitchat that can bore the Knowledge Seeker. Although the Knowledge Seeker may miss the intellectual and abstract discussion they enjoy when they are paired with a Security Seeker, they can obtain their "brain fix" from work colleagues and intellectual friends. The bottom line is that, what they give up in intellectual stimulation when they marry a Security Seeker, they can regain in the form of a satisfying social life, family life, and sex life.

Overall, this combination can work well in the home—both are orderly, meticulous, efficient, and eager to maintain a stable family life. They can also make a good business team since the Knowledge Seeker is technically skilled and inventive, while the Security Seeker is good at managing and executing the ideas.

Here's a chart that summarizes their main differences:

KNOWLEDGE SEEKER	SECURITY SEEKER
Abstract	Concrete
"If I believe it, I'll see it"	"If I see it, I'll believe it"
Respects authority and tradition if it fits within their schema	Respects authority, custom, and tradition
Intellectual and bookish knowledge	Practical and concrete knowledge
Likes deep conversations	Enjoys small talk
Intense	Relaxed, but dutiful
Skeptical	Realistic pessimism

Security Seeker Combination
Security Seeker (SJ) with Meaning Seeker (NF)

Security Seekers share the Meaning Seeker's concern for society and morality of behavior, as well as their desire to do the right thing and help other people.

Moreover, Security Seekers admire the Meaning Seeker's quest for spiritual development and their focus on the potential of things (this differs from the Security Seekers down-to-earth approach to life).

From their viewpoint, the Meaning Seeker is attracted to the Security Seeker's dependability and self-assurance. Security Seekers think concretely, carefully, and cautiously—then they act decisively. They construct meticulous schedules and deadlines to get things done in a precise and thorough manner. In sum, the Security Seekers provide the secure world in which the Meaning Seeker can comfortably make family decisions and navigate their internal world.

The Security Seeker has a firm view of the world and their place in it—deep introspection (the kind favored by the Meaning Seeker) doesn't interest them very much. Although the Security Seeker may not understand the Meaning Seeker's constant need for a deep connection, they do appreciate the Meaning Seeker's emotional depth. And, the Meaning Seeker will be glad to make a heartfelt connection to a partner they feel will be loyal for the long-haul.

Additionally, the optimistic, enthusiastic, lively, and curious Meaning Seeker can energize the calmer, less curious Security Seeker—bringing in fresh ideas and energy.

The challenge in this pairing comes when the Security Seeker is critical of the Meaning Seeker's eternal search for deep meaning and feeling. They fear that the Meaning Seeker can get so carried away by an idea that they may break with tradition and jeopardize the safety and security of their family life. At the same time, the Security Seeker can be annoyed and frustrated by the Meaning Seeker's constant insistence for them to increase the depth, meaning, and emotional connection in their relationship. For a while the Security Seeker may try to satisfy the Meaning Seeker's thirst for more in-depth conversation; but at some point, the Security Seeker will get fed up with their partner's foolish obsession with analyzing the psychological nuances of their lives together. For the pragmatic Security Seeker, the way to improve the relationship is to improve the practical aspects of their everyday family life—not to discuss some theoretical or philosophical ideas about relationships.

Here's a chart that summarizes their main differences:

SECURITY SEEKER	MEANING SEEKER
Biggest fear is being considered irresponsible or inappropriate	Biggest fear is disharmony
I love my family	I want to feel close
Searches for security	Searches for meaning
Practical	Imaginative
Calm, not as curious	Optimistic and enthusiastic
Adheres to tradition	Breaks with tradition for the greater good
Interested in everyday matters of living	Deeply introspective and philosophical

Excitement Seeker Combination
Excitement Seeker (SP) with
Security Seeker (SJ)

Although they seem to be opposites, the Excitement Seeker and Security Seeker can make for an interesting complementary pair. The calm, controlled, cautious Security Seeker is often attracted to the energetic, explosive, risk-taking Excitement Seeker. While the Excitement Seeker "spreads seeds" (initiates new activities, ventures, businesses, lifestyle choices), the Security Seeker can "manage the harvest" (plan, organize, and schedule things so they run smoothly).

For the Security Seeker, the Excitement Seeker can be like a fun, playful child they can take care of—someone who can also be a wonderful diversion (and source of pleasure and relaxation) from their constant working and organizing of everyday matters (their "nose to the grindstone" disciplined life). They also enjoy the Excitement Seeker's vitality and sense of adventure, especially in the sexual arena (exploring new positions, toys, or locales).

On the other hand, the Excitement Seeker sees the cautious and ultra-responsible Security Seeker as a fixed center for their footloose way of life—as a nester who can build the secure home that the Excitement Seeker needs so they can roam free, while knowing they have somewhere (and someone) to come back to. They also get a kick out of loosening up (and teasing) the Security Seeker with their zany, impulsive sense of fun ("Let's take tango lessons; try that bizarre food at the foreign restaurant; have a snowball fight").

On the downside, the Security Seeker can become annoyed with what they view as the Excitement Seeker's sometimes childish, impulsive, and irresponsible behavior. From their Excitement Seeker's perspective, they can see their Security Seeker's persistence as being boring, stubborn, and stuck in their ways.

Another issue that can arise is that they disagree on how to spend their spare time: Security Seekers like to do familiar things, while Excitement Seekers crave the new (adventures, trips, activities). Also, because Excitement Seekers can be socially fun-loving and playful, the Security Seeker may mistake their friendliness to a stranger at a party as being unfaithful to them, or at the least disrespectful, especially when they appear to give too much attention to an attractive person at the social event ("I was just being friendly," says the Excitement Seeker).

Although they have their challenges, this pairing does have its strengths: The Excitement Seeker's positive and flexible outlook on life can bring joy to the Security Seeker, and help them feel better during challenging times. In the meantime, the Excitement Seeker can appreciate the Security Seeker's loyalty and strength of character.

Here's a chart that summarizes their main differences:

EXCITEMENT SEEKER	SECURITY SEEKER
Spontaneous	Structured
Messy and/or disorganized	Neat and organized
Late	On time
Likes spur of the moment activities	Hates surprises and spur of the moment activities
Likes to try new things	Likes the comfort of the tried and true
Can meet people anywhere, spontaneously	Likes to meet people in structured situations or through personal contacts
Biggers fear is losing freedom or being trapped	Biggest fear is being socially judged as irresponsible and inappropriate

Making Differences Work in Your Relationship

Although "opposites attract" may be a misnomer, it does occur, and sometimes it can work out quite well in relationships. The key is to make sure that you thoroughly understand the differences you and your partner have, and that you respect and appreciate those differences (instead of trying to change them).

When you do this, you have an opportunity to develop a complementary relationship in which each of you brings talents and characteristics that the other doesn't have. This can create a very powerful synergistic relationship in which you combine your resources to help each other in areas where each of you is weakest (an organizer with a fun, spontaneous partner). As long as you can embrace each other's differing styles, you will be able to develop a satisfying relationship that stands the test of time.

Chapter 10:
Putting it All Together: Your Blueprint for Finding Love

You have all the tools you need now to find your ideal GuyType, the love of your life. To recap, let's take a look at what you need to do to find the man you're looking for, step by step.

Step One: Know Your LoveTemperament.

Based on the results from Chapter Two, write down your LoveTemperament:

I am a _____, also known as (Put your letters here)_____.

Example: I am a <u>Security Seeker</u>, also known as an <u>SJ</u>.

Step Two: Determine Who Your Most Compatible GuyType Is

You are typically looking for someone who is similar to you. Although dating outside your type is an option (See Chapter Nine), you will do usually better in a long-term relationship if you are with someone who matches your own love style.

I am looking for a _____, also known as (Put his letters here)_____.

Example: (If you are a Security Seeker):

I am looking for a <u>Security Seeker</u>, also known as an <u>SJ</u>.

Step Three: Use Personality Networking (GuyTyping) to Meet Your Ideal Guy

At this point, you have several options to meet your compatible GuyType. You can join personality networks (online and off) that cater to the GuyType you're looking or, you can GuyType him as you run across him in your everyday life (ask him questions or make observations to determine his romantic style), or you can enlist other people (Affinity Wings) to help you.

Start by asking yourself these questions:

*What is my ideal GuyType like on a daily basis?** Let's say you're looking for a brainy Knowledge Seeker, and you want to compare your prototype (Knowledge Seeker) with the men you run across in your life. You further ask yourself:

What are his physical appearance and nonverbals like?

_____

E.g., (for Knowledge Seeker): Uses clothes for comfort and utility. If Introverted, may have rumpled look; if Extraverted, may have a "power look." Uses hand gestures to express the need for precision and control.

What is his personality like?

_____

E.g., (for Knowledge Seeker): Powerful, witty, argumentative, sarcastic, intelligent, competent, blunt, dominant, interested in science, innovation, technology, and achievement.

Where do I find him?

_____

I can find a (Knowledge Seeker) at:

_____

E.g., Activities and groups related to science, technology, education, law, business, politics, upscale events and environments.

Action Step: Pick three fun or interesting activities, groups, or events you can participate in this month to meet your Knowledge Seeker.

In this month, I will:

_____

_____

_____

E.g., Attend a computer fair, join a meetup group about day trading, attend a Facebook event for Star Wars fans (if you really like Star Wars).

*Who do I already know who may be (my ideal GuyType, for example, Knowledge Seeker)?** Write down all of the interesting single men you know—coworkers, friends, acquaintances, men you've bumped into, or heard about in your circle. Write down his name and your best estimate of his GuyType personality (Knowledge Seeker, and so forth), including any other details about him that might give you clues. You can also brainstorm with your friends, and see if they know someone too.

I think these single and available men may be (your ideal GuyType, e.g., Knowledge Seeker):

_____

_____

_____

E.g., Bob, Facebook friend for six months, engineer, always talking about gadgets, has an absent-minded professor look, looks adorable in glasses.

Step 4: Date Him and Win His Heart for a Long-Term Relationship

Now that you've identified the type of man you want, and have information about where to meet him, your last step is to break the ice and develop a winning relationship with him.

Write down ways you can flirt with him and break the ice, depending on his GuyType (e.g., Knowledge Seeker).

I can text or message him things like:

_____

_____

_____

E.g., (for the Knowledge Seeker): "Have you read any good books lately?" "I can beat you in (challenge him to play a game)." "I believe… (mention a topic you strongly believe in and let the debate begin)."

Write down ways in which you can develop affinity and affection based on his GuyType:

To win his heart, I should:

_____

_____

_____

E.g., (for the Knowledge Seeker): Engage him in deep theoretical discussions; partake in witty banter and sarcasm; join him at educational events (book signings, seminars, talks, workshops)

It's Time to Find Your GuyType

Now, it's your turn to go out in the world and GuyType the men you meet, so you can eventually find the love of your life. You will screen out incompatible dates and find the man who will resonate with you at every level—the most compatible long-term mate who will help bring happiness and joy to your life.

I wish you the best of luck and success in your journey, and may your path to love be wide and fulfilling.

Appendix:
ONLINE RESOURCES TO MEET
YOUR IDEAL GUY

Here are some online resources that can help you meet your compatible match. You greatly increase your chances of meeting your ideal guy by getting involved in groups and communities that have a higher percentage of the particular GuyType you're looking for.

Good luck on your search:

EXCITEMENT SEEKER

1. http://museum.oas.org/ - **AMA | Art Museum of the Americas'** work is based on the principle that the arts are transformative for individuals and communities.
2. http://www.americansforthearts.org/- **Americans for the Arts** is the nation's leading nonprofit organization for advancing the arts and arts education.
3. http://fineartamerica.com/ - **Fine Art America** has hundreds of online groups for visual artists.
4. http://usregionalarts.org/ - **Regional Arts Organization** offers funding and programs to serve the arts sector and communities in their member states.
5. http://www.collegeart.org/- **CAA** includes among its members, those who by vocation or avocation are concerned about and/or committed to the practice of art, teaching, and research of and about the visual arts and humanities. Over 12,000 artists, art historians, scholars, curators, critics, collectors, educators, publishers, and other professionals in the visual arts belong as individual members
6. https://www.arteducators.org/ - **National Art Education Association** is the leading professional membership organization exclusively for visual arts educators.

7. http://www.conservation.org/ - **Conservation International** recognized as a financially accountable and transparent organization.

8. http://www.nature.org/ - The **Nature Conservancy** is a conservation organization working around the world to protect ecologically important lands and waters for nature and people.

9. http://www.worldwildlife.org/ - **World Wildlife Fund** is a conservation organization, WWF works in 100 countries and is supported by more than one million members in the United States and close to five million globally.

10. http://www.nwf.org/ - The **National Wildlife Federation** is a nationwide federation of state and territorial affiliate organizations and nearly six million members and supporters across the country.

11. http://www.sierraclub.org/ – The **Sierra Club** is an environmental organization —with more than two million members and supporters.

12. http://wilderness.org/ - The **Wilderness Society** is a conservation organization working to protect our nation's shared wildlands.

13. https://www.craftandhobby.org/ - **CHA** is an international, not-for-profit trade association consisting of thousands of member companies engaged in the design, manufacture, distribution and retail sales of products in the craft and hobby industry.

14. http://www.americancraftspirits.org/ - The **American Craft Spirits Association** is a registered non-profit trade group representing the U.S. craft spirits industry.

15. http://www.acscny.org/ - The **Arts and Crafts Society of Central New York** is a non-profit organization dedicated to the study of the Arts and Crafts Movement through a schedule of lectures, symposia, tours and other educational programs for the purpose of increasing awareness of this rich cultural heritage, and stimulating interest in its preservation.

16. http://www.capitalhikingclub.org/ - **CHC** is a non-profit hiking group who welcomes the public to join them on all hikes.

17. https://www.nyramblers.org/ - The **New York Ramblers** hiking club offers long, strenuous hikes, at a moderate-to-fast pace, for experienced hikers.

18. http://www.bajshc.org/ - **Bay Area Jewish Singles Hiking Club** plans a variety of interesting events for enjoying the outdoors throughout the Bay Area and meeting people in a relaxed, informal way. Participants are single Jews from around the Bay.

19. http://www.highsierrahikers.org/ - The **High Sierra Hikers Association (HSHA)** is a nonprofit, all-volunteer organization formed in 1991 by a handful of concerned hikers.

20. https://outdooradventureclub.com/ - The **Outdoor Adventure Club (OAC)**, the Bay Area's FIRST activity club, run by professional guides, where you can choose from a variety of fun things to do every weekend.

21. www.adventureclubsd.com/ - The **Adventure Club San Diego**: If you're single, Adventure Club San Diego hosts frequent events to meet other eligible adventurers.

22. http://www.standupcomedyclinic.com/ **Stand Up Comedy Clinic:** Whether you want to perform standup comedy, write for other comedians, write sitcoms, greeting cards or humorous filler pieces for magazines and newspapers, the Stand-Up Comedy Clinic can give you the tools to make that a reality.

23. www.arcaracing.com/ - **Automobile Racing Club of America**: a Midwest-based sanctioning body for stock car auto racing.

24. https://www.scca.com/ - **Sports Car Club of America:** A motorsports club in the United States.

25. https://gunowners.org/ - **Gun Owners of America (GOA)** is a non-profit lobbying organization formed in 1975 to preserve and defend the Second Amendment rights of gun owners.

26. https://www.nationalgunrights.org/ - **National Association for Gun Rights**.

27. https://home.nra.org/ - The **National Rifle Association.** With 5 million members, they are protectors of the Second Amendment.

28. https://tastebuds.fm/ - **Tastebuds** connects you with people nearby who have the most in common with you. You can share your favorite music and songs to start meeting new people.

29. http://www.songkick.com/ - **Songkick** connects some of the world's greatest artists with millions of music fans around the globe.

30. http://www.percheronhorse.org/ - The **Percheron Horse Association of America** is a nonprofit corporation dedicated to the preservation and promotion of the purebred Percheron Horse.

31. http://www.usshba.org/ - The **United States Sport Horse Breeders Association (USSHBA)** was created to strengthen the presence and recognition of breeders throughout the US sport horse community.
32. http://www.amha.org/ - The **American Miniature Horse Association** is a Miniature Horse registry with over 200,000 horses registered and more than 10,000 members in 38 countries and provinces.
33. http://www.comedycellarclasses.com/ - **Comedy Cellar Classes.**
34. usadance.org/- **USA Dance Inc** is the National Governing Body for DanceSport in the United States, and with more than 150 chapters throughout the country, is also the representative organization for all social and recreational ballroom and Latin dancers in America, ranging from preschoolers to seniors.
35. www.cordance.org - The **Congress on Research in Dance** is an international organization of dance scholars, educators, and artist that aims to strengthen the visibility and increase the reach of dance as embodied practice, creative endeavor, and intellectual discipline.
36. http://paradoxsports.org/ - **Paradox Sports** is rooted in the power of the climbing community.
37. www.usesa.org/ - The **United States Extreme Sports Association** represents Extreme Sports Communities, Participants, and Enthusiasts.
38. adacs.org - **Adaptive Action Sports** creates skateboard and other action sort camps, events, and programs for youth, young adults, and wounded veterans living with permanent physical disabilities, TBI, and PTSD.
39. http://www.immaf.org/ - **International Mixed Martial Arts Federation:** The international democratic governing body for the sport of MMA, representing stakeholders worldwide – athletes, coaches, referees, governments, athletic commissions, sports confederations, international associations, professional promoters and more.
40. camo-mma.org/- **California Amateur Mixed Martial Arts Organization, Inc.** (CAMO), is a non-profit corporation dedicated to help foster the growth of the sport of amateur Mixed Martial Arts and to oversee the health, safety and welfare of the athletes that choose to participate in it.

41. https://usafootball.com/ **USA Football** champions the athletes, parents, coaches, officials and administrators who bring youth and scholastic football to life.

42. http://www.lasvegas.com/things-to-do/ - The **LVCVA** is the official destination marketing organization of Las Vegas and the surrounding Clark County Area.

43. http://www.atlanticcitynj.com/explore/ The **CRDA**'s goal is to attract visitors over the age of 21, including **Atlantic City** tours, conventions, meetings, business travel and leisure travel who will spend their time in Atlantic City.

44. http://www.miamiandbeaches.com/places-to-see/south-beach-art-deco-district - **South Beach** has been called the American Riviera and an Art Deco Playground. Yet there's more than fine white sand and colorful buildings to South Beach's fantasy-land of exuberant Deco architecture.

45. http://www.mardigrasneworleans.com/ - **Mardi Gras New Orleans:** The Greatest Free Show on Earth.

46. http://www.esquire.com/food-drink/bars/a44780/best-bars-in-america/ - **18 Best Bars in America;** putting together a list of America's best bars.

47. https://www.nasp.com/ - **NASP** This association was created for people who are serious about their sales career. People who want to grow. People who understand that their time is the most precious thing they have.

48. https://www.smei.org/ - **SMEI:** A global sales and marketing professional association. Members enjoy online forums, educational webinars and peer connections for knowledge sharing.

49. http://www.bni.com/ - **BNI:** A business referral organization.

50. https://www.aact.org/ - **American Association of Community Theatre:** Helping theatres thrive, with expertise, assistance, networking & support to help create the best possible experience for participants & audiences alike.

51. http://www.hellohola.org/ - **HOLA** strengthens and supports the available talent pool through its professional educational services and awards for excellence in theater.

52. http://www.actorsfund.org/ -The **Actors Fund:** A national human services organization here to meet the needs of our enter-

tainment community with a unique understanding of the challenges involved in a life in the arts.

53. http://smhsociety.org/ - The **SMH Comedy Society** is a non-profit organization that runs Stand Up for Mental Health programs in the Vancouver area.

54. http://www.lightsupimprov.com/ - **Lights Up** Business and Organization Workshops immerse participants in the improvisor's world, as they learn to see how the "improvisational attitude" applies to their own specific areas of professional leadership and care giving.

55. http://www.iaaglobal.org/ - **International Advertising Association** have over 3,000 individual members across corporate, marketing services, organizational and academic sectors – all involved in the branding, communications and marketing disciplines.

56. https://oaaa.org/ - **OAAA** protects, unites, and advances the interests of the OOH advertising industry.

57. https://www.iab.com/ - **IAB** advocates for its members and promotes the value of the interactive advertising industry to legislators and policymakers.

58. https://www.ama.org/ - The **American Marketing Association** (AMA) is a community for marketers.

59. http://www.sportsmarketingnetwork.com/ - **National Sports Marketing Network** (NSMN) is the trade organization for the sports business industry in the United States.

60. http://www.sempo.org/ - **SEMPO** is a global non-profit organization serving the search engine marketing industry and marketing professionals engaged in it. Purpose is to provide a foundation for industry growth through building stronger relationships, fostering awareness, providing education, promoting the industry, generating research, and creating a better understanding of search and its role in marketing.

61. https://www.anmp.com/ - The **Association of Network Marketing Professionals** (ANMP) is an association uniting Network Marketing professionals' worldwide —distributors, company owners and executives, as well as strategic partners of the Network Marketing community.

SECURITY SEEKER

1. http://familiesusa.org/- **Families USA** is a nonprofit, nonpartisan consumer health advocacy organization.
2. http://www.familyvoices.org/ - **Family Voices** is a national, nonprofit, family-led organization promoting quality health care.
3. www.boundless.org/ - **Boundless is** an award-winning ministry of Focus on the Family with the goal of helping young adults grow up, own their faith, date with purpose, and prepare for marriage and family.
4. http://www.nari.org/ - **NARI** is an organization of remodeling professionals.
5. http://www.hiri.org/ - The **Home Improvement Research Institute** (HIRI) is a membership based, independent, not-for-profit organization of manufacturers, retailers, wholesalers and allied organizations in the home improvement industry.
6. http://www.aarp.org/ - **AARP's** mission is to enhance the quality of life for all as they age.
7. http://www.acei.org/ - **ACEI** works for the education of all children, but has a special interest in ensuring that our energies are focused on meeting the education needs of the most fragile and vulnerable children.
8. http://www.feedthechildren.org/ - **Feed the Children** exists to end childhood hunger.
9. http://www.bgca.org/ **Boys & Girls Clubs** programs and services promote and enhance the development of boys and girls by instilling a sense of competence, usefulness, belonging and influence.
10. https://www.children.org/- **Children International** works with organizations around the world to better the lives of children in poverty.
11. http://www.hopeforpaws.org/ - **Hope for Paws** helps animals who suffer and die every year because of negligence and abuse.
12. http://bestfriends.org/ - **Best Friends Animal Society** nonprofit organization, operates a sanctuary for homeless animals; provides adoption, spay/neuter, and educational programs.
13. https://petpartners.org/ - **Pet Partners** is a nonprofit registering handlers of multiple species as volunteer teams providing Animal-Assisted Interventions.

14. https://www.aspca.org/ - The **American Society for the Prevention of Cruelty to Animals®** (ASPCA®) was the first humane society to be established in North America and is, today, one of the largest in the world.

15. http://www.ncpc.org/ - **Neighborhood Watch** brings citizens together with law enforcement to deter crime and make communities safer.

16. https://www.hands.org/ - **All Hands Volunteers** is a volunteer-powered disaster relief organization dedicated to Rebuilding Hope for people impacted by natural disasters all over the world.

17. http://www.pta.org/ - **PTA** is a voice for all children, a relevant resource for families and communities, and a strong advocate for public education.

18. http://www.singleparentadvocate.org/ - **Single Parent Advocate**, a local 501(c) 3 non-profit organization providing resource connections, growth-based training, and support for single parent families, based in Dallas, Texas and the surrounding areas.

19. http://www.parentswithoutpartners.org/ - **PWP** is the largest international, nonprofit membership organization devoted to the welfare and interests of single parents and their children.

20. http://www.spaoa.org/ - **SPAOA** is a forum for information and resources for single parents across America, as well as a place for members to interact and provide support and advice to each other throughout the site itself.

21. https://www.goldmedalwineclub.com/ - The **Gold Medal Wine Club** searches for small production, award-winning wines from California and the world's best boutique wineries and delivers them direct to wine enthusiasts across the country.

22. http://www.winemonthclub.com/ - The **International Wine of the Month Club** was founded and continues to be run on Principles dedicated to consistently delivering quality, variety, and value through our stringent wine selection process.

23. http://lacountyfair.com/ **Los Angeles County Fair** is about community, agriculture, and education.

24. http://www.usapatriotism.org/ - **USA Patriotism!** is a site about showcasing pride for the United States of America in a "nonpolitical" environment with a mission to foster pride of America by

her citizens and a better understanding about the USA from citizens of other countries.

25. mfvsoa.org/ - **Military Family and Veterans Service Organizations of America (MFVSOA)** is a federation of America's finest national organizations working to ensure our military and their families are not forgotten in their service and sacrifice.

26. www.iccwbo.org/ - **ICC** the world business organization, a representative body that speaks with authority on behalf of enterprises from all sectors in every part of the world.

27. https://www.rotary.org/- **Rotary International** is an international service organization whose stated purpose is to bring together business and professional leaders to provide humanitarian services, encourage high ethical standards in all vocations, and to advance goodwill and peace around the world.

28. www.lionsclubs.org/ - **Lions Clubs International:** The World's Largest Service Club Organization.

29. www.kiwanis.org/ - **Kiwanis clubs** are located in 80 nations, and help their communities.

30. http://www.ymca.int/ - **YMCA** is a worldwide organization based in Geneva, Switzerland, with more than 57 million beneficiaries from 125 national associations.

31. http://www.nrpe.org/- The **National Religious Partnership for the Environment** is an alliance of four religious organizations and institutions committed to caring for God's Creation. The Partnership is supported by individual, church, and organizational donations.

32. https://www.unicef.org - **UNICEF** works with other agencies to make sure that children are on the global agenda.

33. http://www.petmeds.org/ - **PetMeds®** supports pet rescue and adoption.

34. http://theshelterpetproject.org/- **The Shelter Pet Project** is the result of a collaborative effort between two leading animal welfare groups, The Humane Society of the United States and Maddie's Fund, and the leading producer of public service advertising (PSA) campaigns, The Ad Council.

35. http://tnbainc.org/ - The **National Bowling Association, Inc.** is a non-profit corporation organized in August 1939, in Detroit,

Michigan, for the express purpose of encouraging African-Americans to develop their skills in the game of Ten Pins.

36. https://www.aclu.org/ - The **American Civil Liberties Union (ACLU)** is a nonpartisan, non-profit organization [5][6] whose stated mission is "to defend and preserve the individual rights and liberties guaranteed to every person in this country by the Constitution and laws of the United States."

37. www.clubforgrowth.org/- The **Club for Growth** is a national network of over 100,000 pro-growth, limited government Americans who share in the belief that prosperity and opportunity come from economic freedom.

38. http://www.algonquingolfclub.com/ - **Algonquin Golf Club** is a private golf club located in the heart of the St. Louis, Missouri Metropolitan area.

39. https://lwvc.org/ - The **League of Women Voters**, a nonpartisan political organization, which encourages informed and active participation in government, works to increase understanding of major public policy issues, and influences public policy through education and advocacy.

40. http://www.wfo-oma.com/ - **WFO, the World Farmers Organization**, is an International Organization of Farmers for Farmers, which aims to bring together all the national producer and farm cooperative organizations with the objective of developing policies which favor and support farmers' causes in developed and developing countries around the world.

41. http://ifmaonline.org/ - The **International Farm Management Association** is a society of people who are involved directly or indirectly in the agricultural process and who have an interest in the agriculture of other parts of the world than their own.

42. thesinglegourmet.net/ - The **Single Gourmet** is a premier social dining and travel club.

43. https://www.volunteerforever.com/ - **Volunteer Forever's** goal is to be the most trusted resource in the world for volunteering abroad.

44. http://www.culinaryschools.org/international/ - **Culinary Schools** for culinary students.

45. http://membership.usta.com/ - The **United States Tennis Association (USTA)** is the national governing body for the sport of

tennis and the recognized leader in promoting and developing the sport's growth on every level in the United States, from local communities to the crown jewel of the professional game, the US Open.

46. https://www.fhi360.org - **FHI 360** is a nonprofit human development organization dedicated to improving lives in lasting ways by advancing integrated, locally driven solutions.

47. https://asq.org/ - **ASQ** provides training, professional certifications, and knowledge to a vast network of members of the global quality community.

48. The **Watchmen** are a group of benefactors who have come together with their own individual talents, knowledge, resources, and expertise, to form an organizational support system for all official Watchmen Groups and Individual Patriot Citizens across the nation.

49. http://patrioticmillionaires.org/ - The **Patriotic Millionaires** is a group of high-net worth Americans who are committed to building a more prosperous, stable, and inclusive nation.

50. https://www.singleparentlove.com/ - **SingleParentLove** is a single parent dating website helping single moms and single dads find their match.

51. http://www.singleparentmeet.com/ - **SingleParentMeet.com** is an online dating service for single parents.

52. http://www.freedatingamerica.com/ - **Free Dating America:** Free Single Parents Dating Site For Moms and Dads.

MEANING SEEKER

1. http://www.apa.org/ - **APA** is the leading scientific and professional organization representing psychology in the United States, with more than 117,500 researchers, educators, clinicians, consultants and students as its members.

2. https://www.socialpsychology.org/ - **SPN** is an educational organization with over 1,000 members worldwide.

3. https://www.siop.org/ - **SIOP** is a membership organization for those practicing and teaching I-O psychologies.

4. http://www.psychologicalscience.org/ - The **Association for Psychological Science** (previously the American Psychological

Society) is a nonprofit organization dedicated to the advancement of scientific psychology and its representation at the national and international level.

5. http://hartleyfoundation.org/ - The **Hartley Film Foundation** is a non-profit organization dedicated to cultivation, support and distribution of the best documentaries and audio meditations on world religions and spirituality.

6. http://www.brahmakumaris.org/ - The **Brahma Kumaris World Spiritual Organization** acknowledges the intrinsic goodness of all people.

7. spiritualallianceusa.org/ - The **National Spiritual Alliance**.

8. www.acpaweb.org/ - **ACPA** is an organization of Catholic philosophers established in 1926 to promote the advancement of philosophy as an intellectual discipline consonant with Catholic tradition.

9. https://environmentalphilosophy.org/ - **IAEP** is a philosophical organization focused on the field of environmental philosophy.

10. https://www.amphilsoc.org - the **American Philosophical Society** promotes useful knowledge in the sciences and humanities through excellence in scholarly research, professional meetings, publications, library resources, and community outreach.

11. https://www.fisp.org - **FISP** is an International Federation of Philosophical Societies, whose member-societies arguably include every country where there is significant academic philosophy.

12. www.iheu.org - **IHEU** is an umbrella organization of humanist, atheist, rationalist, secular, skeptic, free thought and Ethical Culture organizations worldwide.

13. **ACS** has worked to save lives and create a world with less cancer.

14. www.heart.org/ - The **American Heart Association** is the nation's oldest and largest voluntary organization dedicated to fighting heart disease and stroke.

15. www.greenpeace.org - **Greenpeace** is an independent global campaigning organization that acts to change attitudes and behavior, to protect and conserve the environment, and to promote peace.

16. https://www.icrc.org/ - The **International Committee of the Red Cross** (ICRC)—ensuring humanitarian protection and assistance for victims of war and other situations of violence.

17. www.savethewhales.org/ - **Save the Whales!** Our purpose is to educate children and adults about marine mammals, their environment, and their preservation.

18. https://www.peacecorps.gov - The **Peace Corps** is a service opportunity for motivated change makers to immerse themselves in a community abroad, working side by side with local leaders to tackle the most pressing challenges of our generation.

19. www.naacp.org/ - The mission of the **National Association for the Advancement of Colored People** (NAACP) is to ensure the political, educational, social, and economic equality of rights of all persons, and to eliminate race-based discrimination.

20. http://www.gop.com/ - The **Republican Party.**

21. https://www.democrats.org/ - The **Democratic Party.**

22. www.amfar.org/ - The **American Foundation for AIDS Research**, a leading organization dedicated to the support of HIV/AIDS research.

23. www.humanesociety.org - The **Humane Society of the United States** is the nation's largest and most effective animal protection organization.

24. www.bbbs.org/- **Big Brothers Big Sisters of America** mentoring organization in the United States, volunteers provide support and advice to youth. Information on joining, local chapters, donations, news and stories.

25. www.churchleadership.org/ - **Church Leadership:** Thinking and Providing Biblical and Grace-Centered Theological Resources for the Church.

26. www.pfaw.org/ - **People For the American Way (PFAW)** is a progressive advocacy group in the United States.

27. http://www.citizensincharge.org/ - **Citizens in Charge** is a 501 (c) (4) citizen-powered advocacy organization that serves as a partner to Citizens in Charge Foundation in protecting and expanding the initiative and referendum process.

28. www.commoncause.org - **Common Cause:** Nonprofit, nonpartisan citizen's lobbying organization promoting open, honest, and accountable government.

29. earthfirstjournal.org/ - **Earth First!** is a radical environmental advocacy group that emerged in the Southwestern United States in 1979.
30. www.afj.org/ - **AFJ** works to ensure that the federal judiciary advances core constitutional values, preserves human rights and unfettered access to the courts, and adheres to the even-handed administration of justice for all Americans.
31. https://anthonyrobbinsfoundation.org - The **Anthony Robbins Foundation** is a non-profit organization created to empower individuals and organizations to make a significant difference in the quality of life of people often forgotten—youth, homeless and hungry, prisoners, elderly and disabled.
32. www.landmarkworldwide.com/ - **Landmark Worldwide** is an international personal and professional growth, training and development company—a global educational enterprise committed to the fundamental principle that people have the possibility of success, fulfillment, and greatness.
33. www.lls.org/ -**Leukemia & Lymphoma Society:** Non-profit organization fighting blood related cancers including leukemia, lymphoma, and multiple myeloma.
34. https://www.toastmasters.org/ - **Toastmasters International:** Non-profit organization developing public speaking and leadership skills through practice and feedback in local clubs since 1924.
35. www.nsaspeaker.org/ - **National Speakers Association:** Resources and networking opportunities for professional speakers.
36. http://booksigningevent.com/- **Book Signings and Events** in the U.S.
37. http://www.ala.org/conferencesevents/celebrationweeks - The **American Library Association** (ALA) is the oldest and largest library association in the world.
38. www.ifla.org/ - The **International Federation of Library Associations and Institutions** (IFLA) is an international body representing the interests of library and information services and their users. It is the global voice of the library and information profession.
39. https://iynaus.org/- **IYNAUS:** Search for certified teachers by state, become a member, and access links to yoga resources.

40. https://www.yogaalliance.org/ -**Yoga Alliance**® is a nonprofit association representing the yoga community. Their mission is to promote and support the integrity and diversity of the teaching of yoga.

41. www.vasishtayoga.org/- **VYRF** conducts yoga courses, workshops, seminars, holistic yoga therapy, and many other trainings and educational workshops concerning the deeper science of Yoga.

42. newearthevents.com/ **New Earth Events:** They produce events all over California, including New Earth Expo, Holistic Living Expo, and Psychic and Healing Arts Fair.

43. www.bodymindspiritdirectory.org - **Body Mind Spirit Events** have Holistic Health Expos, Psychic Fairs, Trade Shows, Retreats, Conferences and Travel Opportunities that cover Body Mind Spirit, Natural Healing, Nutrition, Organics, Green Lifestyles, Wellness, Yoga, Sustainability, Self-Reliance, Conscious Living, Metaphysics, Faeries, Gems, Beads, Whole Foods, Gluten Free Lifestyles, Spirituality, and Inspiration.

44. http://www.holisticfestivaloflife.com/ **Holistic festival of life and wellness.** Meet specialists licensed in western medicine whose focus is geared toward holistic living. They have many renowned doctors with specialties in family health, fertility medicine, and who offer various other skilled wellness services.

45. http://newlivingexpo.com/ - **New Living Expo**: A line-up of speakers, i.e., best-selling authors, indigenous elder wisdom, and scientific thought.

46. http://bodysoulspiritexpo.com/ The **Body Soul & Spirit Expo** showcases products, services and resources for growth, and fosters the individual quest for wholeness and self-understanding.

47. https://newlifeexpo.com/ - **New Life Expo:** For Health, Rejuvenation, and Enlightenment.

48. http://spirituallifeproductions.org/ **Austin Metaphysical & Holistic Life Expo** Spiritual Life Productions Co-Creates Educational Holistic, Spiritual and Metaphysical Fairs.

49. https://www.learninglight.org/ - **Learning Light Foundation**: Staff and Volunteers continue to carry on the Light of serving the Community with Integrity, Love, and Compassion. Creating an Open and Safe Environment for All to Gather and Share.

50. www.icfj.org - The **International Center for Journalists** (ICFJ) is at the forefront of the news revolution. Our programs empower journalists and engage citizens with new technologies and best practices.
51. http://www.topeventsusa.com/ **Top Events in all USA** features some of the main events.
52. http://www.ippanetwork.org/ **Positive psychology** is a new field of inquiry that has captured the interest of thousands of researchers, practitioners, and students from around the world.
53. http://www.cpapsych.org/ The **California Psychological Association** (CPA) is a 501(c)(6) non-profit professional association for licensed psychologists and others affiliated with the delivery of psychological services.
54. http://www.isps.org/ - **ISPS** is an international organization promoting psychotherapy and psychological treatments for persons with psychosis (a term which includes persons diagnosed with "schizophrenia").
55. http://www.apadivisions.org/ - **Div. 49** is an organization that welcomes all psychologists interested in the study and application of group dynamics.
56. http://spiritualnaturalistsociety.org/ - **Spiritual Naturalist Society** exists to help bring Spiritual Naturalists together for mutual learning, growth, encouragement, and fellowship.
57. https://spiritualcareassociation.org/ - The **Spiritual Care Association (SCA)** is the first multidisciplinary, international professional membership association for spiritual care providers that establishes evidence-based quality indicators, scope of practice, and a knowledge base for spiritual care in health care.
58. http://spiritualprogressives.org/ - The **Network of Spiritual Progressives** welcomes secular humanists, atheists and people who are "spiritual but not religious" as well as people from every religious community who share the values of love, generosity, creativity, wonder and a commitment to respect one another.
59. http://vedantin.org/ **American Vedanta** is an inclusive, open-armed spiritual organization built on the principles of Vedanta and focused on expressing them in terms of Western sensibilities and lifestyle. It is about connecting with God in the here and now, and living spiritual practice on a daily basis.

60. http://www.spiritualarts.org/ - **Spiritual Arts Institute**, a metaphysical school for the aura, health and spiritual growth. They offer inspiring workshops and classes, taught in-person and online, designed to build a direct connection to the Divine and ignite the soul's potential.

61. https://renovare.org - **Renovaré USA** is a Christian nonprofit that models, resources, and advocates fullness of life with God experienced, by grace, through the spiritual practices of Jesus and of the historical Church.

62. https://www.spiritualsingles.com/ - **Spiritual Singles**: A spiritual dating site offers spiritual groups, spiritual events, spiritual retreats and workshops for yoga singles, meditation singles, conscious singles, new age singles, and light workers.

63. **EliteSingles** unite like-minded American singles & caters to all races, religions and ages.

64. https://www.dharmamatch.com/ - **dharmaMatch**, a dating/matchmaking site for spiritual singles.

65. http://www.soulfulmatch.com/ - **Soulful Match** spiritual dating site for spiritually-oriented singles offers spiritual groups, spiritual events, spiritual retreats and workshops for yoga singles, meditation singles, conscious singles, new age singles and light workers.

KNOWLEDGE SEEKER

1. http://www.startrek.com/upcoming_events **Star Trek Event:** The exhibition will showcase Star Trek's significant impact on culture, society, arts, sports, technology, fashion and more.

2. https://www.facebook.com/groups/9974403646/ The **Official STAR TREK Convention.** This group has been established to provide a place for people to exchange information about the upcoming Creation Entertainment conventions, as well to share the photos and experiences from those conventions.

3. http://www.starwars.com/events/conventions **Star Wars Convention** click on the events section to find out when and where the next convention will take place. Always in motion the future!

4. www.comic-con.org/ -**Comic-Con International** is a nonprofit educational corporation dedicated to creating awareness of, and

appreciation for, comics and related popular art forms, primarily through the presentation of conventions and events that celebrate the historic and ongoing contribution of comics to art and culture.

5. www.newyorkcomiccon.com/ - **New York Comic Con** is the largest pop culture event on the East Coast. Hosting the latest in comics, graphic novels, anime, manga, video games, toys, movies.

6. https://www.americanbar.org/ - The **American Bar Association** is one of the world's largest voluntary professional organizations, with nearly 400,000 members and more than 3,500 entities.

7. http://www.upcomingcons.com/- **UpcomingCons** is committed to providing the most updated comic con list anywhere.

8. www.aaes.org - The **American Association of Engineering Societies** (AAES) is a multidisciplinary organization of engineering societies dedicated to advancing the knowledge, understanding, and practice of engineering.

9. https://www.nspe.org/ - **NSPE** represents individual engineering professionals and licensed engineers across all disciplines.

10. https://www.asme.org/ - **ASME** (**American Society of Mechanical Engineers**) promotes the art, science & practice of multidisciplinary engineering around the globe.

11. https://www.ieee.org/ - **IEEE** is a "voice" for engineering, computing, and technology information around the globe.

12. www.theiet.org/ - The **Institution of Engineering and Technology:** Professional society for the engineering and technology community, with more than 150000 members in 127 countries.

13. www.feani.org/- **FEANI** is a federation of professional engineers that unites national engineering associations from 34 European Higher Education Area (EHEA) countries.

14. usasbe.org/ - The mission of the **United States Association for Small Business and Entrepreneurship**® is to provide the network to advance knowledge and foster business development through entrepreneurship education and research.

15. www.msuea.org/ - The **Entrepreneurship Association** is an MSU Registered Student Organization for students who are passionate about entrepreneurship and innovation.

16. naeonline.org/ - The **National Association of Entrepreneurship** is a Washington D.C. based organization dedicated to helping the American Entrepreneur.

17. https://www.eonetwork.org/ - The **Entrepreneur's Organization** (EO) is a Global business network of 12,000+ leading entrepreneurs in 160 chapters and 50 countries.

18. www.uiausa.org/ -**United Inventors Association:** A nonprofit organization providing educational resources and opportunities to the inventing community.

19. https://www.ifia.com/ - **IFIA International Federation of Inventors Associations** is the global platform for invention and innovation and invention enthusiasts.

20. www.theiaga.org/ - **The International Association of Gaming Advisors** (IAGA) has provided a relevant, collaborative forum for discussing key issues that affect global gaming today.

21. https://theppa.org/ - The **Poker Players Alliance** (PPA) is the leading non-profit membership organization representing American poker players with the goal of establishing a safe and secure place to play poker.

22. http://www.apcw.org/ - **APCW:** The Association of Players, Casinos, and Webmasters.

23. www.illinoiscasinogaming.org/ **Illinois Casino Gaming Association** coordinates industry initiatives, including advocacy and education on such issues as economic development, community service and responsible gaming.

24. www.tesol.org/ -**TESOL International Association** hosts more than 6,500 people annually from around the world at its convention.

25. www.cecconvention.org/ - the **CEC Convention & Expo**, is the global event for special and gifted education.

26. www.himssconference.org/ - **HIMSS** globally transforms health and healthcare through the best use of IT by driving thought leadership, analytics, community and professional development.

27. https://conference.iste.org/- **ISTE:** Extraordinary educators deserve an extraordinary conference.

28. www.tceaconvention.org/ - The five-day **TCEA Annual Convention & Exposition** is one of the largest educational technology conventions in the nation and the largest in Texas.

29. www.cue.org/ - The **CUE Conference** is the largest and oldest education technology conference in California, and among the largest in the United States.

30. https://www.actfl.org - The **ACTFL Annual Convention and World Languages Expo** is an international event bringing together more than 7,000 language educators from all languages, levels, and assignments.

31. http://www.atlantasymphony.org/ The **Atlanta Symphony Orchestra** and its affiliated members are committed to build on our foundation of artistic excellence.

32. http://www.guitarfoundation.org/ - The **Guitar Foundation of America** is a classical guitar organization in the world. It is a non-profit corporation dedicated to classical guitar performance, literature, and history.

33. http://sfems.org/ - **San Francisco Early Music Society.** A community-based, membership organization dedicated to the advancement of historically-informed performance of early music.

34. jazzeducation.org/ - **Jazz Education Inc.**, sponsors four main programs: The Jazz & Poetry Series, Summer Jazz Workshop, August Jazz Month Houston, Houston International Jazz Festival, and several special projects.

35. www.ijfo.org/ - **IJFO** is an umbrella organization including 16 leading jazz festivals worldwide.

36. www.ispa.org/- **International Society for the Performing Arts:** A nonprofit organization of executives and directors of concert and performance halls, festivals, performing companies, and artist competitions.

37. www.artdealers.org/ - The **Art Dealers Association of America** (ADAA) is a non-profit membership organization of the nation's leading galleries in the fine arts.

38. blueavocado.org/ - **Blue Avocado** is the bimonthly newsletter of American Nonprofits, a membership organization that provides practical financial information and support to U.S. 501(c) (3) nonprofit organizations, staff, stakeholders, and volunteers.

39. https://www.fide.com - **FIDE** is an international organization that connects the various national chess federations around the world, and acts as the governing body of international chess competition.

40. https://www.af4c.org/ - The **AF4C** is a non-profit organization dedicated to strengthening the minds and character of young people by advancing chess in our schools and our culture.

41. http://www.nscfchess.org/ - The **NSCF** is a 501C (3) foundation dedicated to promoting the teaching of chess in the schools.
42. http://thepartyhotline.com/ - **The Party Hotline:** The society of single professionals.
43. https://www.literacyworldwide.org - The **International Literacy Association** (ILA) is a global advocacy and membership organization of more than 300,000 literacy educators, researchers, and experts across 75 countries.
44. http://www.slaviclinguistics.org/ - The **Slavic Linguistics Society** (SLS) supports the international community of scholars and students interested in the systematic and scholarly study of the Slavic languages.
45. www.linguisticsociety.org/ - The **Linguistic Society of America** (LSA) was founded in 1924 to advance the scientific study of language.
46. www.isle-linguistics.org/ - The central aim of **ISLE** is to promote the study of English Language, that is, the study of the structure and history of standard and non-standard varieties of English, in terms of both form and function, at an international level.
47. www.ipsa.org/ - **IPSA** has maintained its links with the United Nations and has supported the development of other international and regional political science organizations.
48. https://www.hg.org - **US Trial Lawyers Associations:** Find comprehensive information about trial lawyer associations in the United States.
49. www.thenationaltriallawyers.org/ The **National Trial Lawyers** is a professional organization composed of the premier trial lawyers from across the country who exemplifies superior qualifications as civil plaintiff or criminal defense trial lawyers.
50. https://founderscard.com/ - **FoundersCard** is a membership community of over 20,000 entrepreneurs, and innovators who receive benefits and networking opportunities.
51. http://www.vistage.com/ - **Vistage's** members attend meetings each month to participate in idea-sharing and advice-giving.
52. https://yec.co/ - **YEC:** A Community for Business Professionals.
53. http://www.ypo.org/ - **YPO** is the global platform for chief executives to engage, learn, and grow. YPO members harness the knowledge, influence and trust of influential and innovative

business leaders to inspire business, personal, family, and community impact.

54. http://tie.org/ - **The Indus Entrepreneurs (TiE),** was founded in 1992 in Silicon Valley by a group of successful entrepreneurs, corporate executives, and senior professionals with roots in the Indus region.

55. http://enactus.org/ - **Enactus:** A community of student, academic, and business leaders committed to using the power of entrepreneurial action to transform lives and shape a better more sustainable world.

56. http://endeavor.org/ - **Endeavo**r is leading the high-impact entrepreneurship movement around the world.

57. https://www.startupgrind.com/ - **Startup Grind** is an independent startup community, actively educating, inspiring, and connecting 400,000 founders in over 200 cities.

58. http://www.tecglobal.org/ - The **Entrepreneurs' Club** is an international multi-ethnic network of several thousand high-tech entrepreneurs, executives, and other professionals started in 2003.

59. https://www.ashoka.org/ -**Ashoka** is a network of social entrepreneurs with over 3,000 members from all over the world. Ashoka provides everything from start-up financing, networking opportunities to professional support systems.

60. https://socialenterprise.us/ - **Social Enterprise Alliance** is the national membership organization and key catalyst for the rapidly growing social enterprise movement in the United States.

61. http://founderdating.com/ - **Founder Dating**: Build relationships and get real advice from entrepreneurs, start-up founders, and company advisers.

About
DR. ALEXANDER AVILA

Dr. Alexander Avila holds four graduate degrees, including a Ph.D. in clinical psychology. He is the bestselling author of *LoveTypes*
(Avon Books) and *The Gift of Shyness* (Simon
and Schuster). *LoveTypes* is the first book to
teach readers how to find their compatible
soul mate from among the 16 Myers-Briggs
personality types. Over 40 million Internet
users have applied Dr. Avila's LoveType system to find lasting love.
The Gift of Shyness has broken new ground by showing shy and Introverted singles how to embrace their Introversion and Shyness to
develop social confidence and attract their ideal love partner.

As a respected college professor, researcher, and presenter, Dr. Avila
has shared his findings with students, academics, and professionals
in the fields of psychology and human behavioral sciences.

An acclaimed TV and Radio Personality, Dr. Avila is the creator of
the award-winning radio program, Love University, in which listen-
ers learn how to love themselves, others, and a higher power. He has
appeared on numerous media outlets such as *CNN, ABC, CBS, and
Telemundo*, and has been featured in *Cosmopolitan, Glamour, Lati-
na, Today's Black Woman, Real Health, Woman's World*, and the *Los
Angeles Times*, among other publications.

On a personal note, Dr. Avila enjoys salsa dancing, chess, books,
good-hearted people, martial arts, animals, nature, and spirituality.

Dr. Avila's mission is to help humanity transform pain into power
and to extend loving energy to the world. Dr. Avila can be reached at
guytypes.com and guytypes4u@gmail.com.

RECEIVE THE FREE EBOOK GIFT
THAT WILL CHANGE
YOUR LIFE:
THE 3 SECRETS OF HAPPINESS:
FOREVER JOY CAN BE YOURS

In mold of *The Alchemist* and *The Teachings of Don Juan*, *The Three Secrets of Happiness: Forever, Joy Can be Yours* by bestselling author and psychologist, Dr. Alexander Avila, inspires you to leave behind what has trapped you and achieve your highest self.

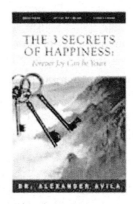

The Three Secrets of Happiness is a modern fable about a pompous psychiatrist, Harry, who goes to interview (for his next bestselling book) a mountain hermit, Tanaka—a mysterious personage who is alleged to know the secrets of happiness. Stubborn and filled with his own hidden pain, the psychiatrist receives more than he bargained for as he comes under the tutelage of the spunky, yet wise, Tanaka. In the end, the psychiatrist abandons his false self and finds peace and love by transforming his destiny through the Three Secrets of Happiness: Gratitude, Joyful Optimism, and Forgiveness.

Now it's your turn: Are you ready to learn the three secrets of happiness and live your heart's desires?

You will never be the same again.

GO HERE FOR YOUR FREE GIFT: "THE 3 SECRETS OF HAPPINESS": http://www.guytypes.com/freegift/

AS AN EXTRA BONUS, YOU WILL RECEIVE A COPY OF MY MONTHLY E-ZINE: "LOVE UNIVERSITY SECRETS": Each month, you will receive the latest research-proven tips, strategies, and findings for achieving self-confidence and finding (and keeping) love in your life. Dr. Avila will be your personal mentor and guide as you learn how to love yourself, others, and the higher possibilities of life.

READ THE BOOK
THAT STARTED THE DATING
REVOLUTION AND FIND YOUR
SOUL MATE TODAY: *LOVETYPES:*
DISCOVER YOUR ROMANTIC
STYLE AND FIND YOUR
SOUL MATE

Now, there's a solution to incompatible dates and failed relationships: It's called *LoveTypes: Discover Your Romantic Style and Find Your Soul Mate* by Dr. Alexander Avila.

With over 40 million followers, and 20 years of proven love compatibility results, *LoveTypes* is your go-to guide to help you find your soul mate from among the crowd of potential suitors. Dr. Avila has revolutionized the dating world by applying the theory behind the *Myers-Briggs Type Indicator®* —the most popular personality test in the world—to teach readers how to find their most compatible partner from among the 16 LoveTypes, or romantic styles. By taking a brief quiz, you first determine your unique LoveType profile. From there, the system guides you toward the best LoveType for you and provides specific answers to your most pressing relationship questions:

*Which of the 16 LoveTypes is most compatible with me—psychologically, emotionally, and sexually?

*What four questions can I ask to determine instantly if someone is right for me?

*Where can I meet my ideal mate?

*What dating strategies will win the heart of my ideal LoveType and ensure a long-term relationship?

Lasting love no longer has to be hit or miss with *LoveTypes*, your complete and indispensable guide to a happy and fulfilling romantic life.

TO FIND YOUR SOUL MATE TODAY, GO HERE:
http://www.guytypes.com/my-books/

Made in the USA
Coppell, TX
27 January 2020

15029004R00095